Paws and Play - A Photobook

Exploring Tender Moments - A Delightful Photobook

By PhotoPydia

"A dog is the only thing on earth that loves you more thanhe loves himself."

—Josh Billings

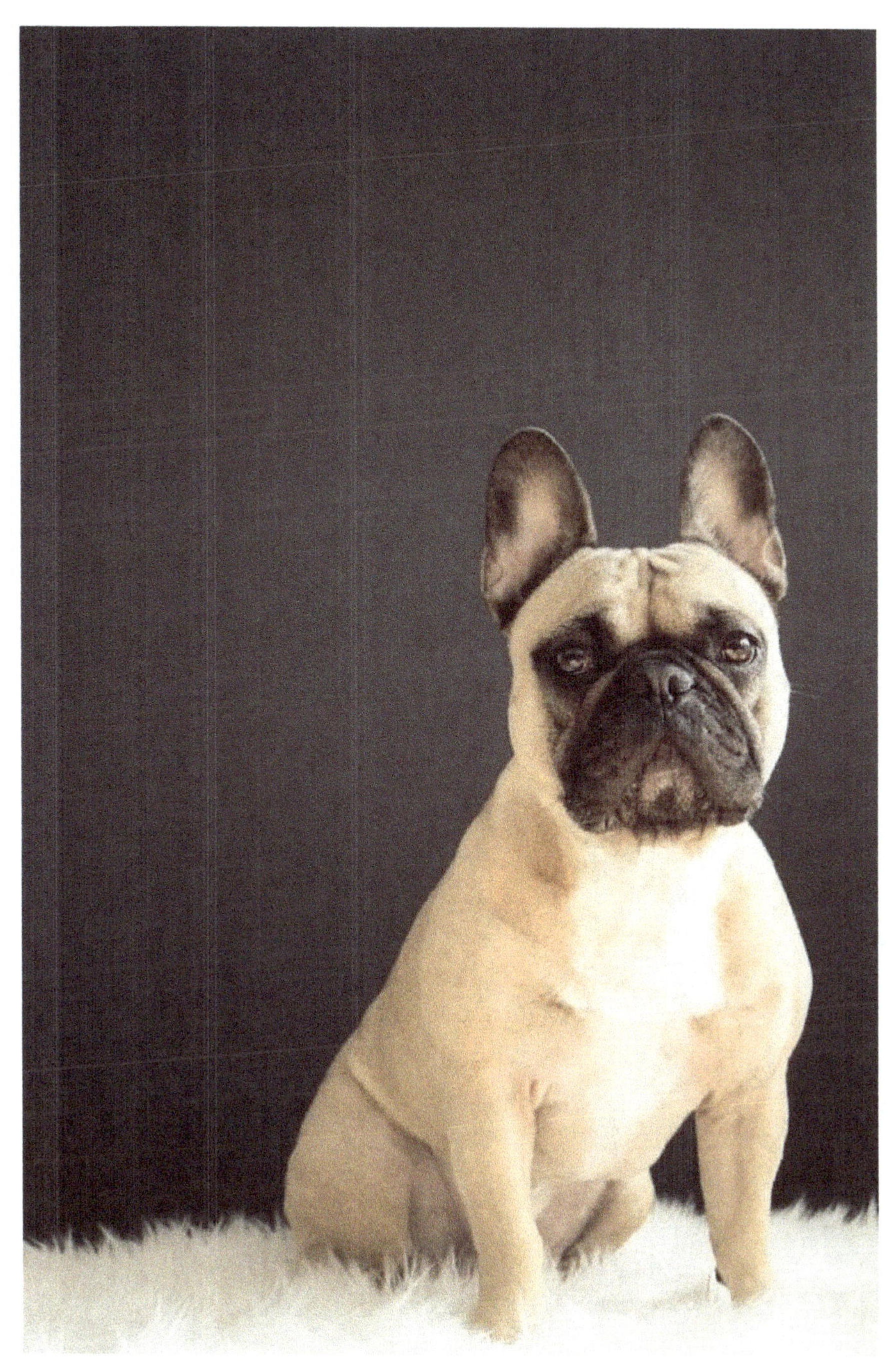

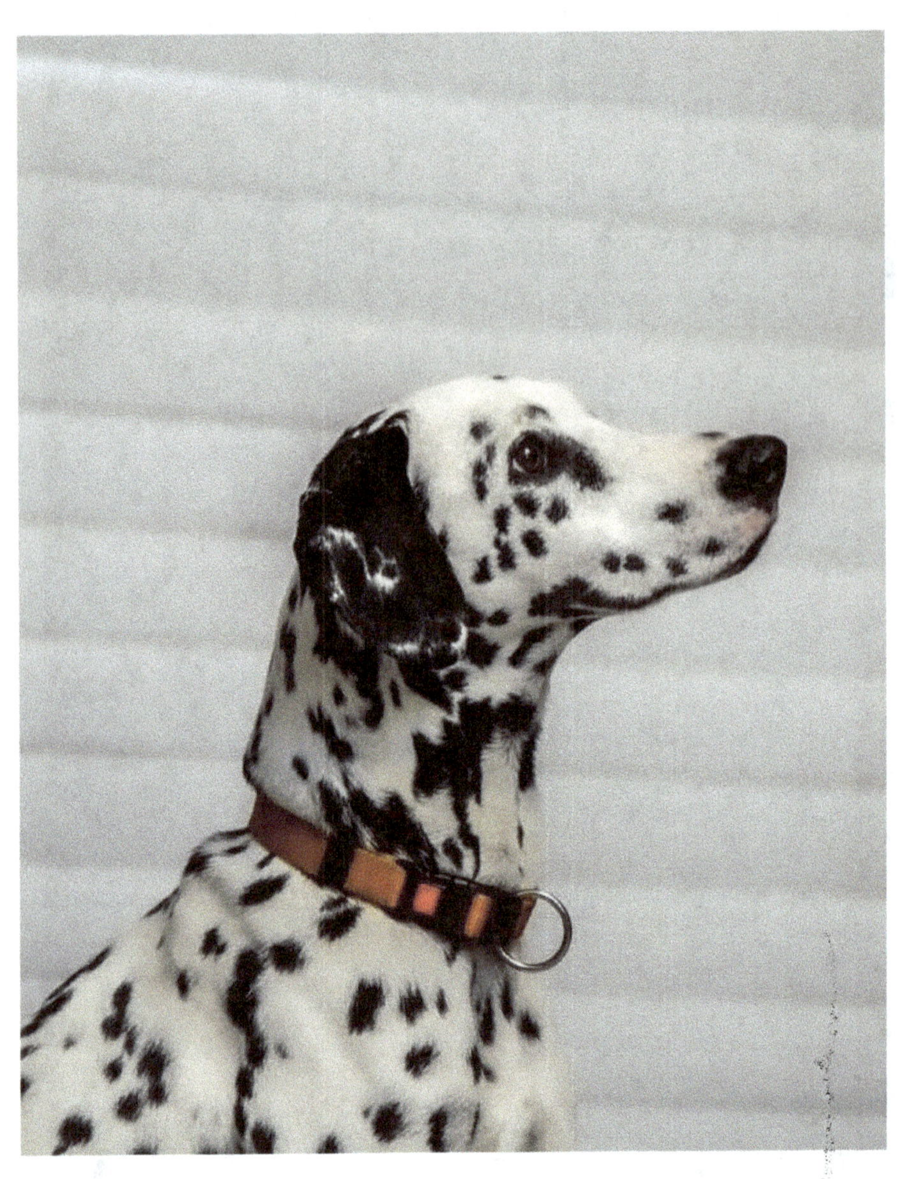

4

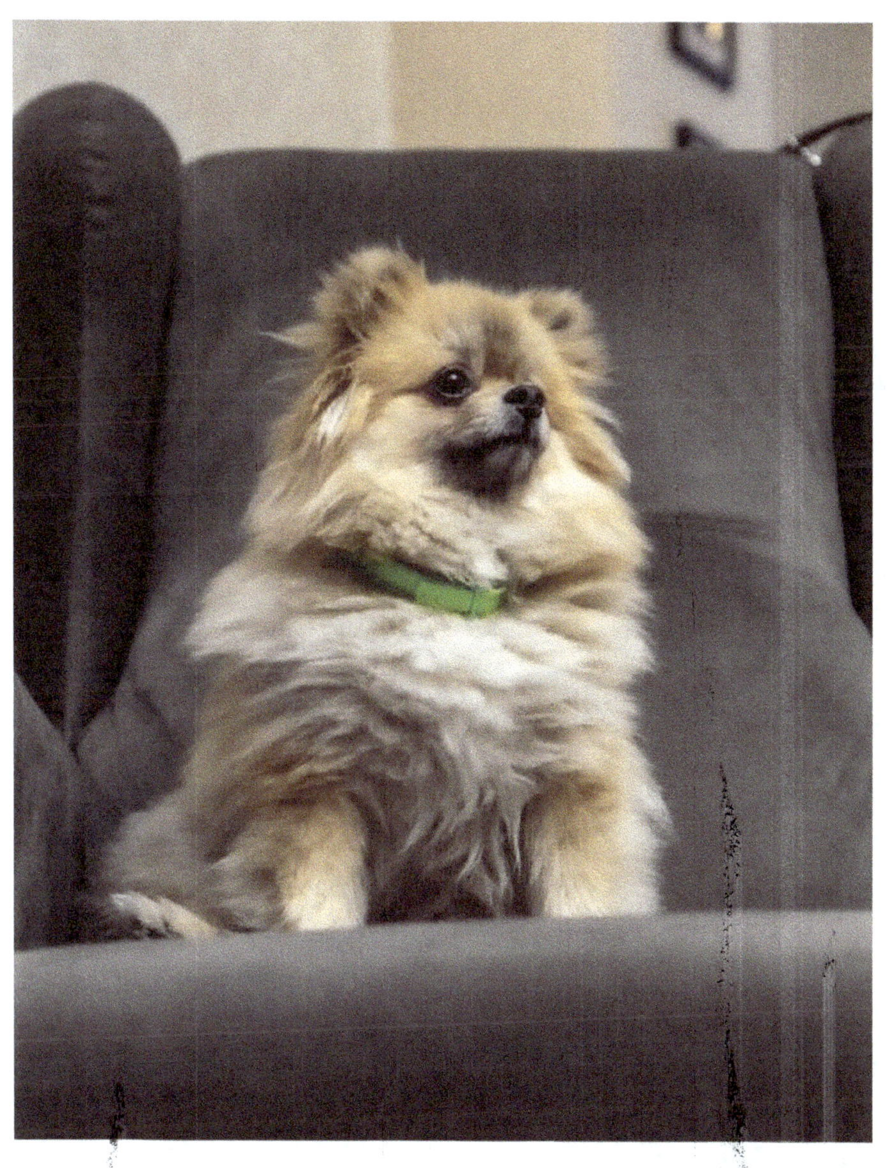

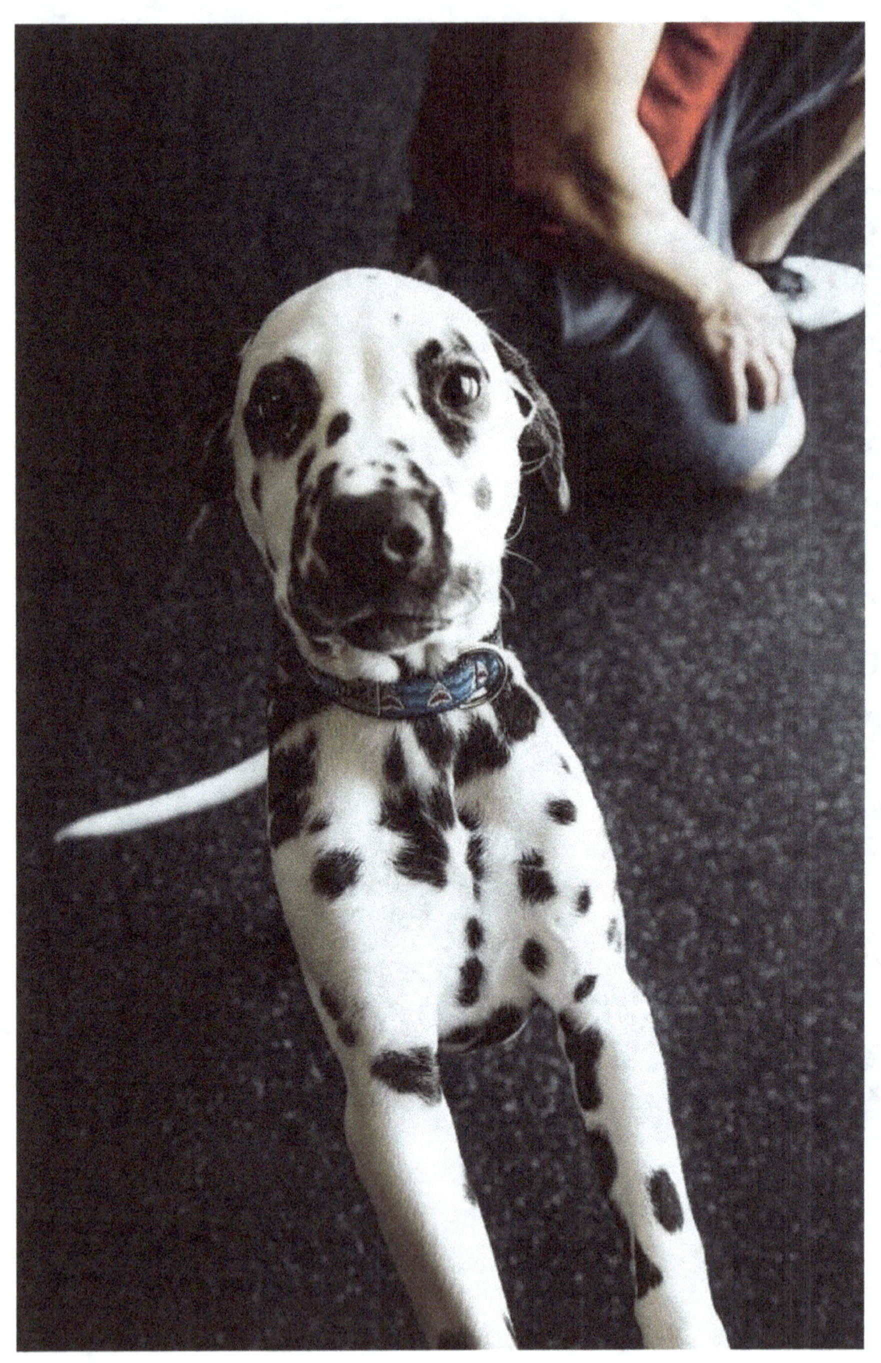

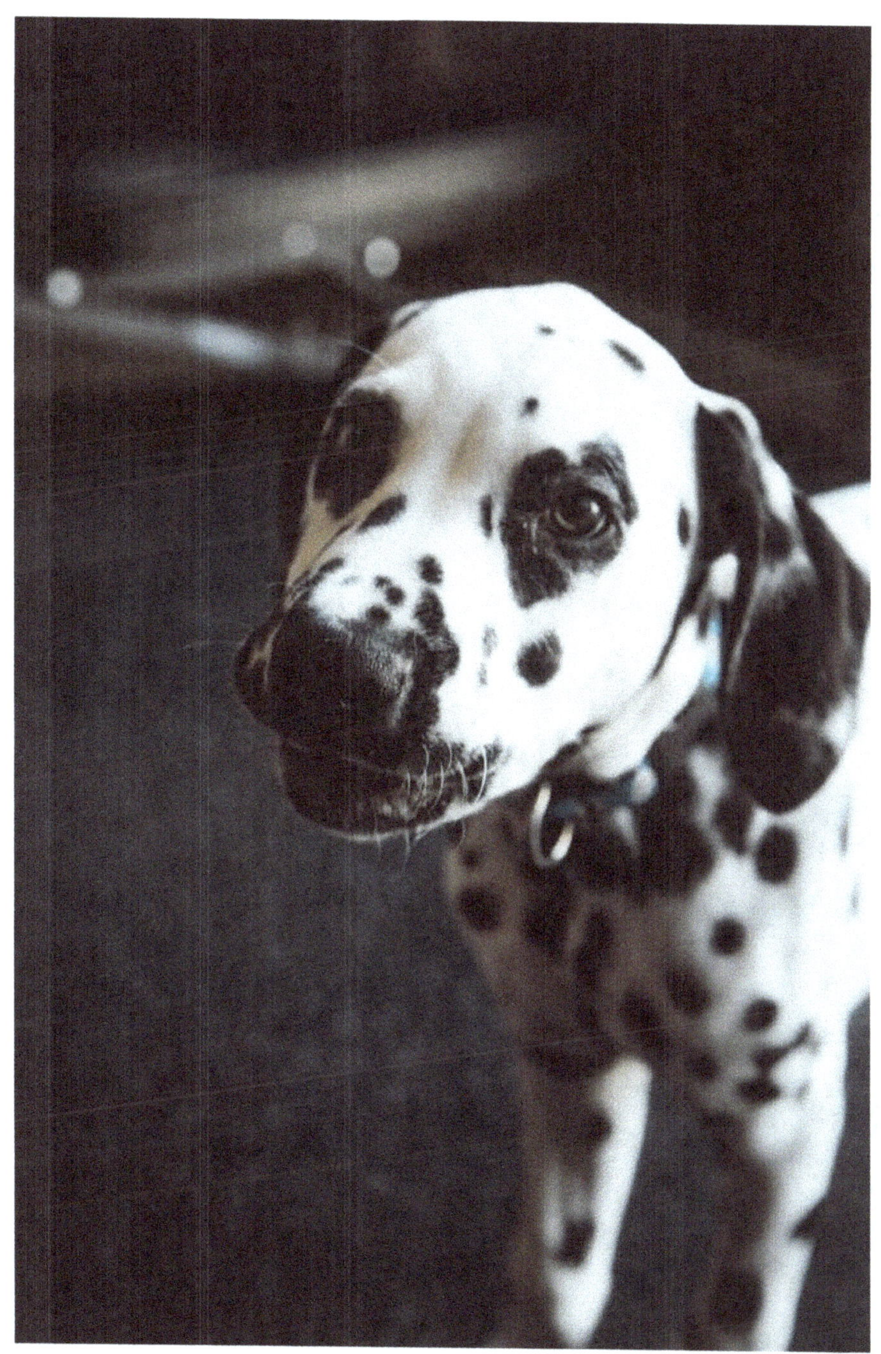

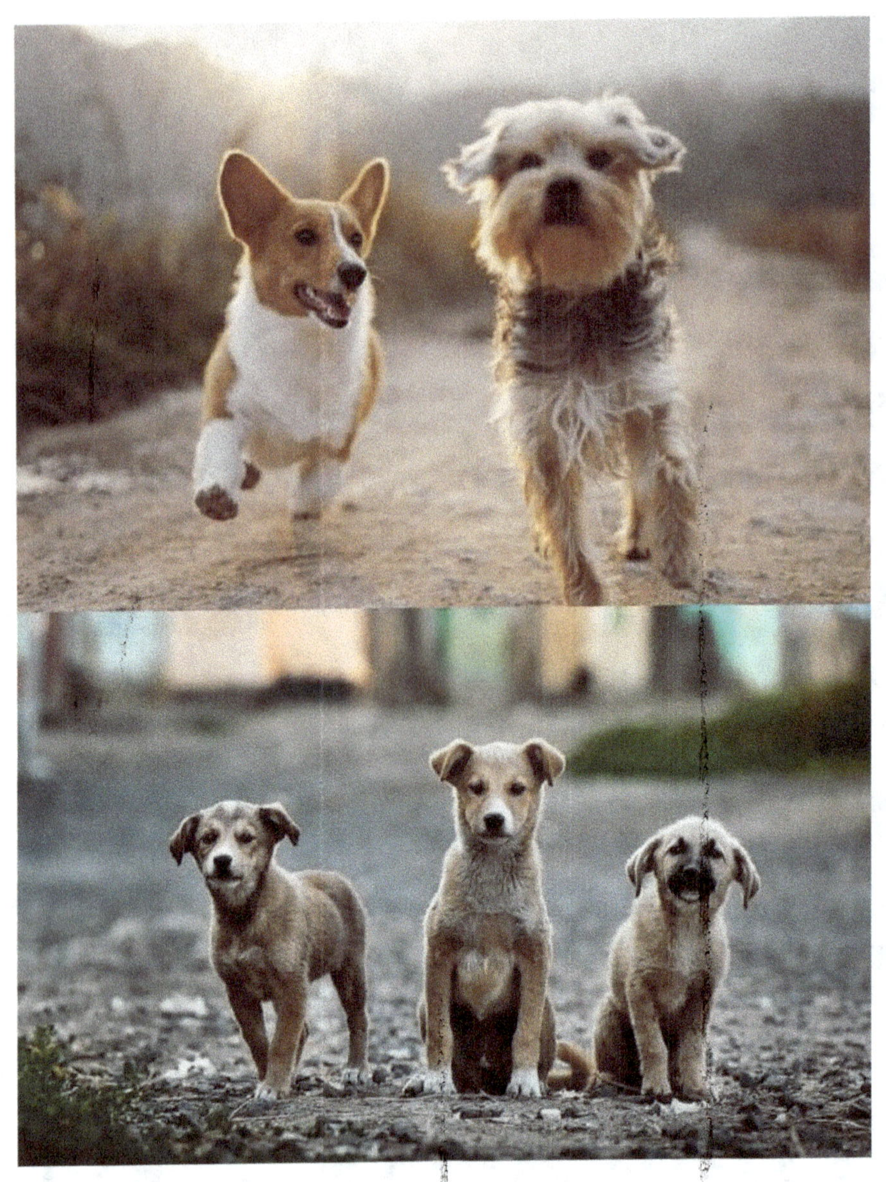

8

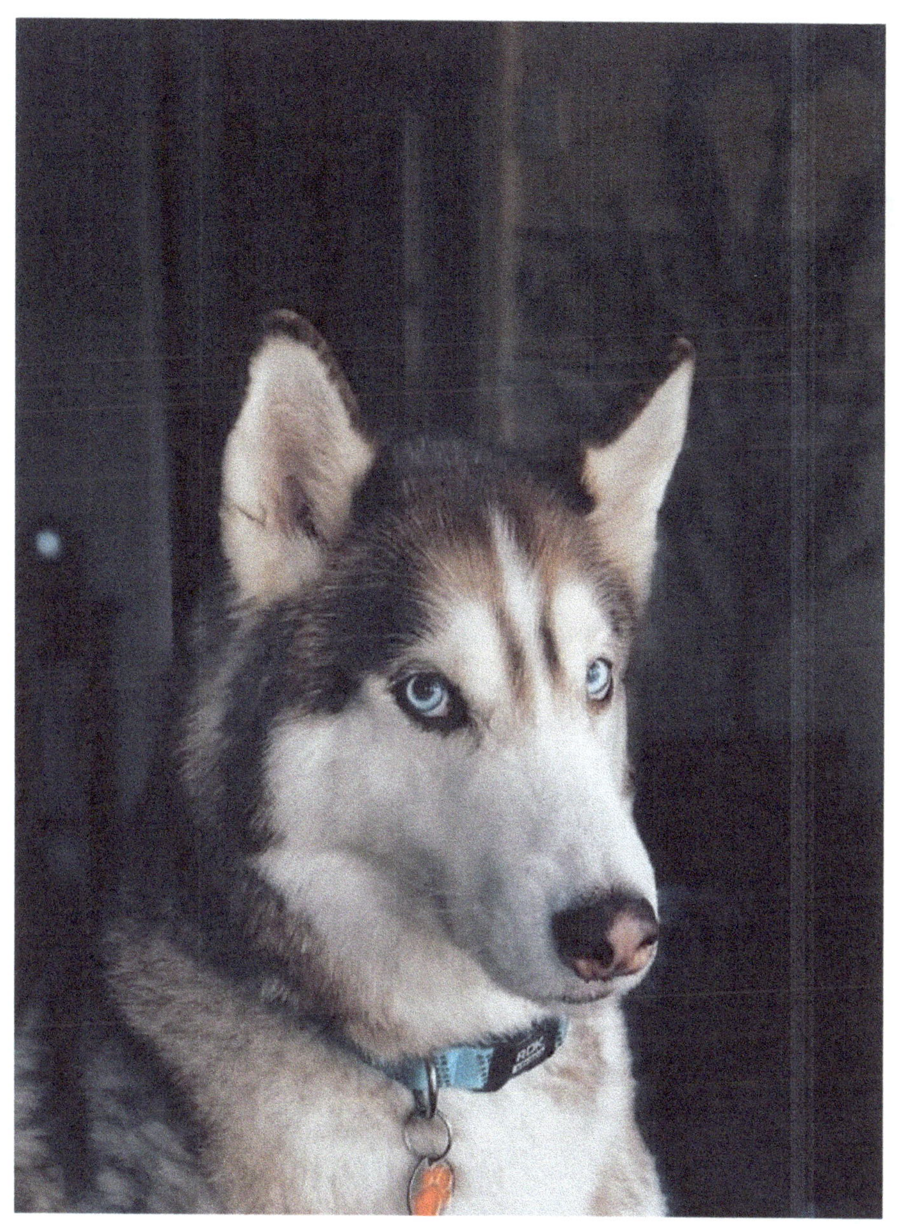

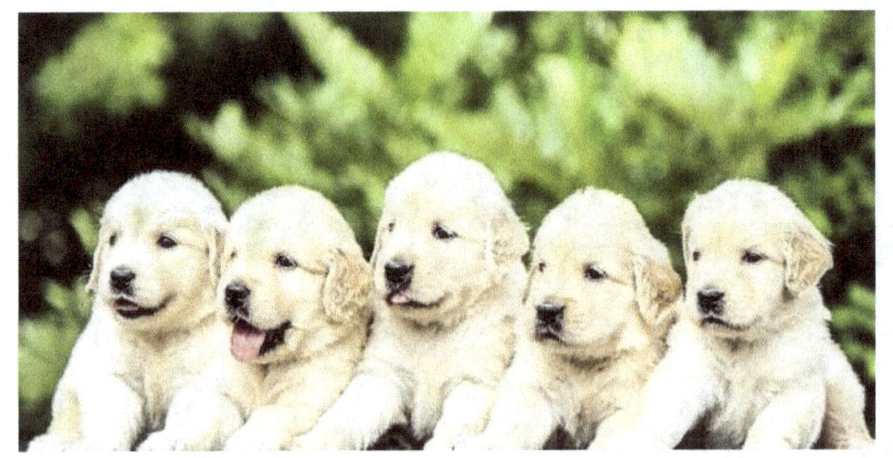

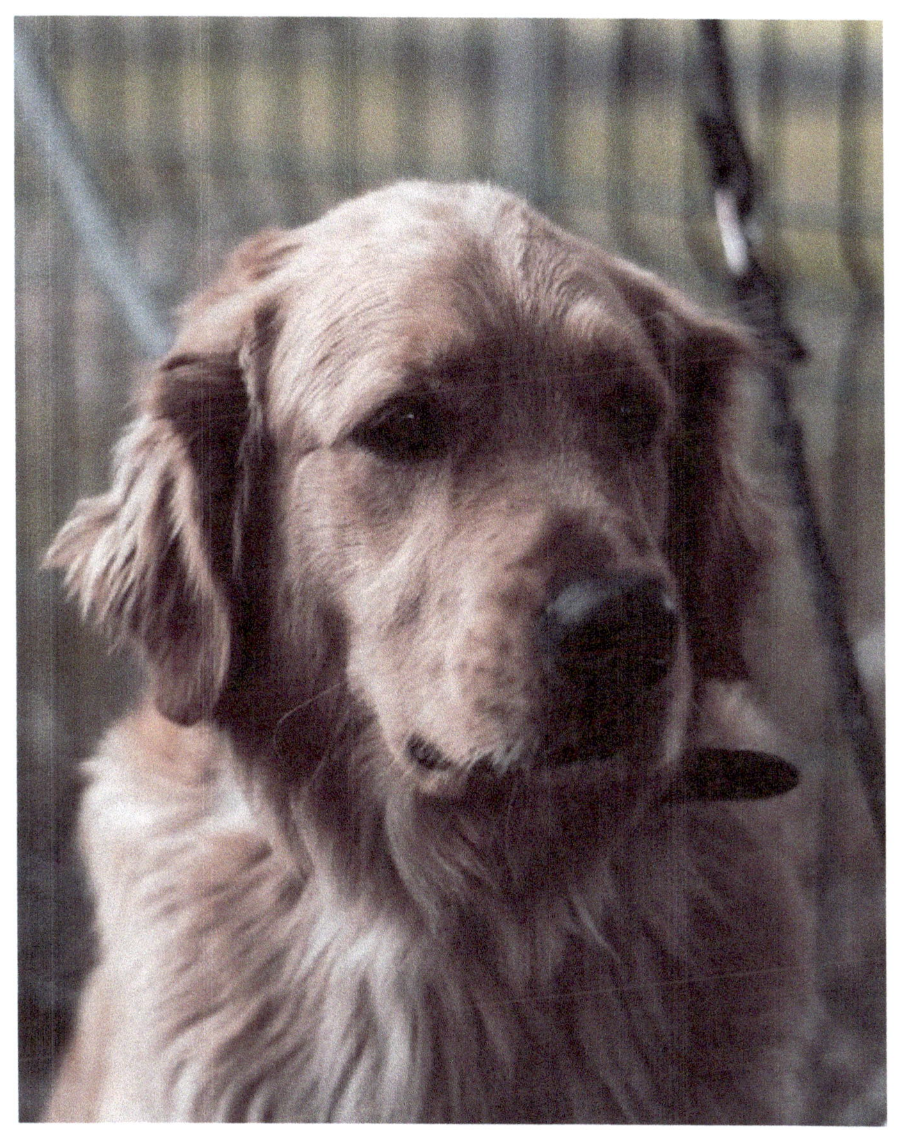

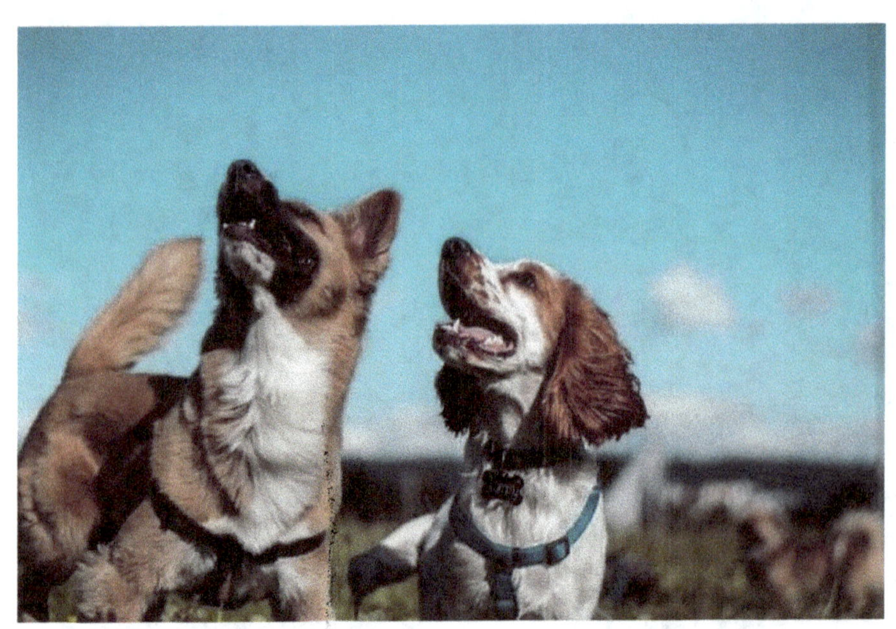

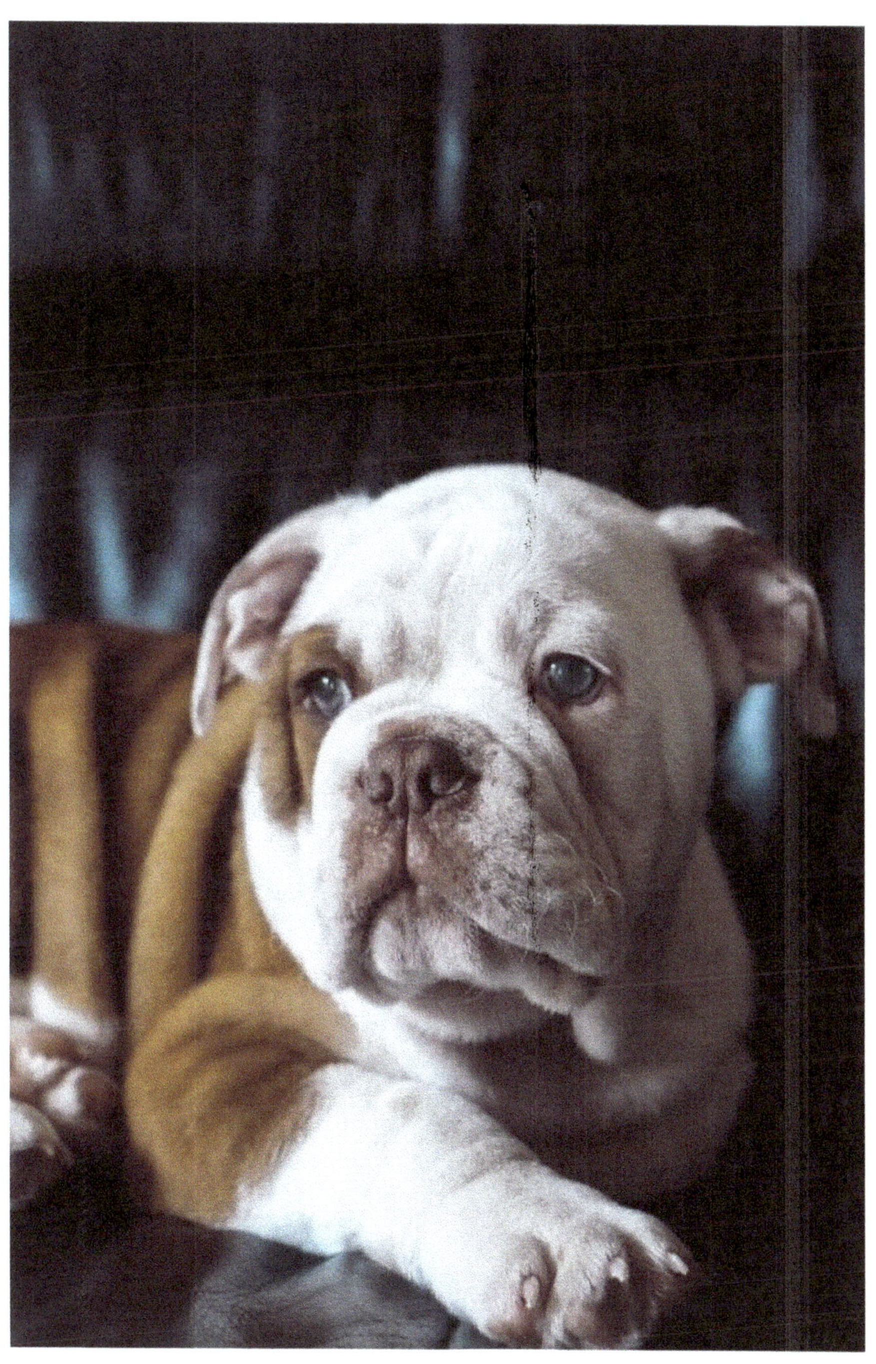

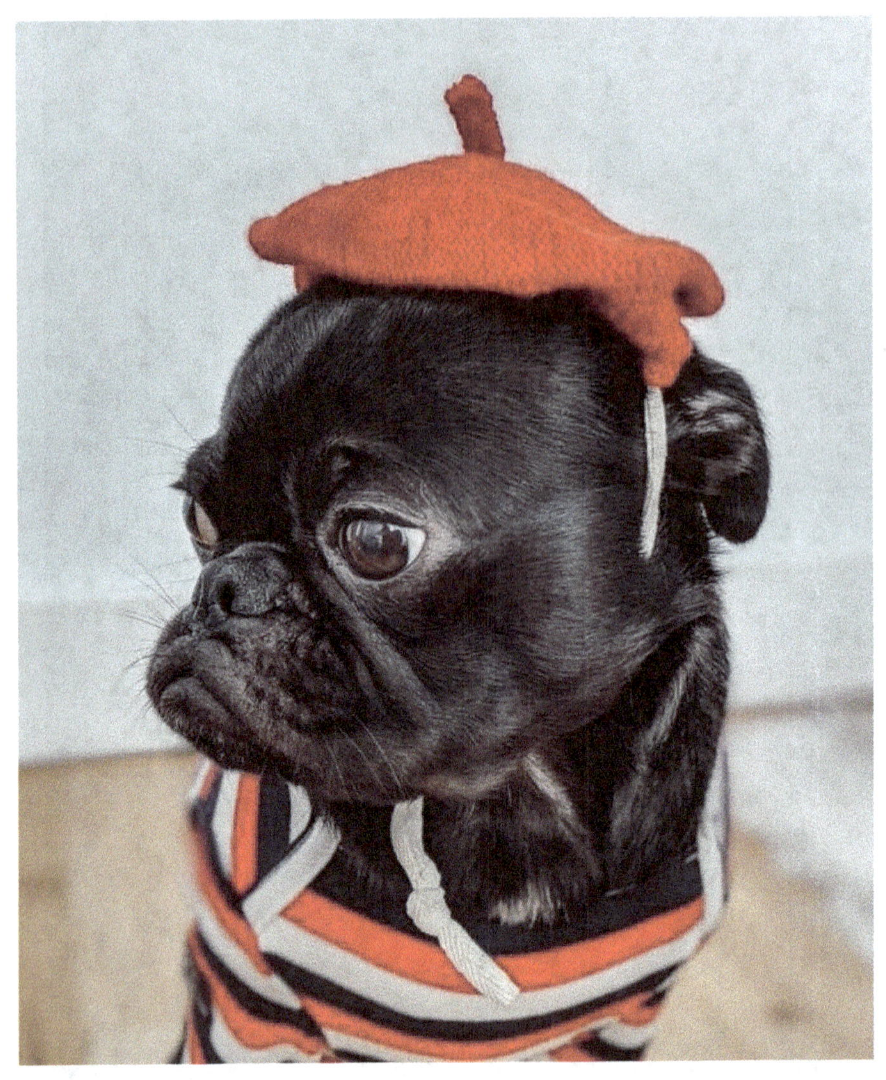

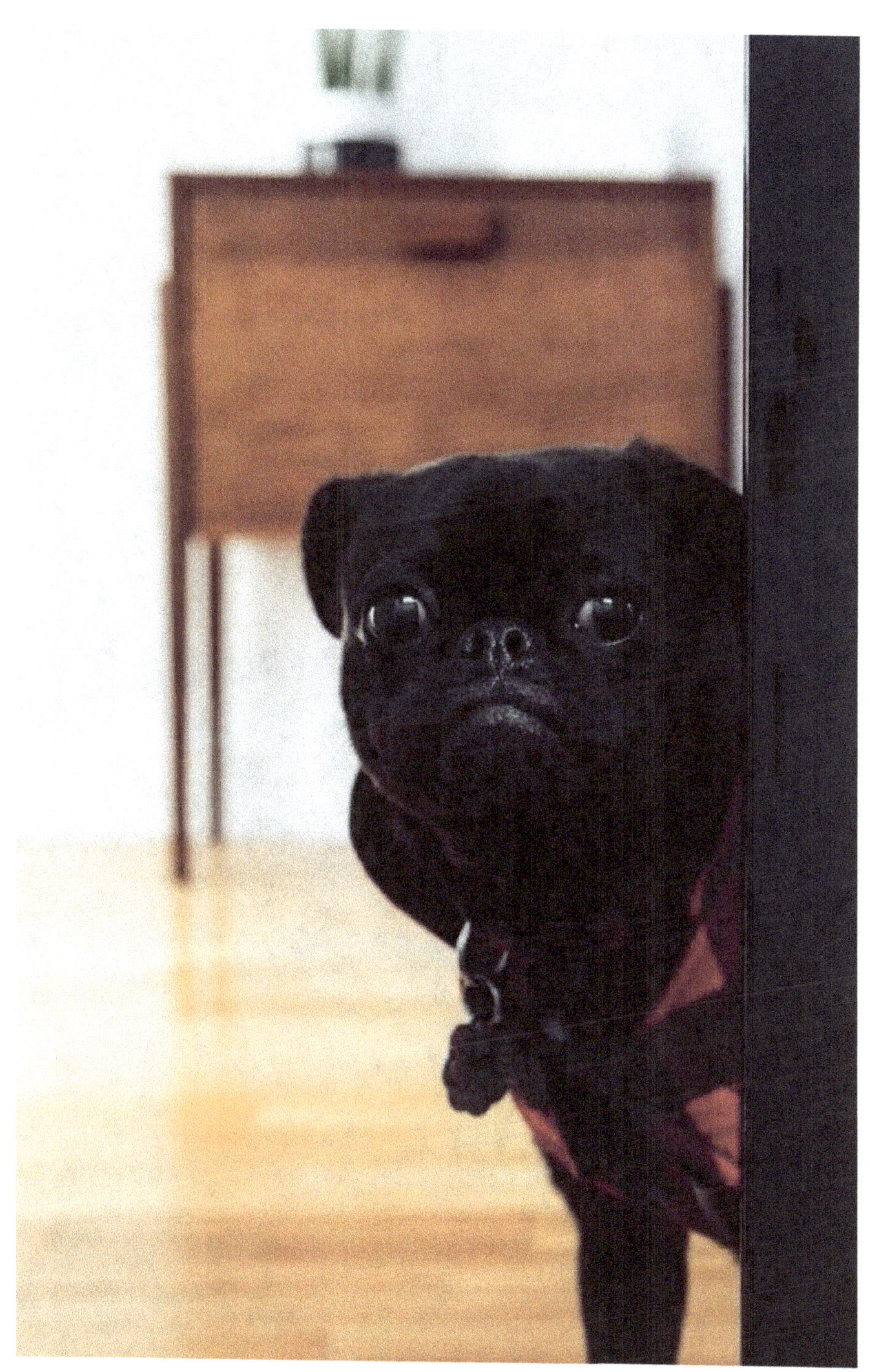

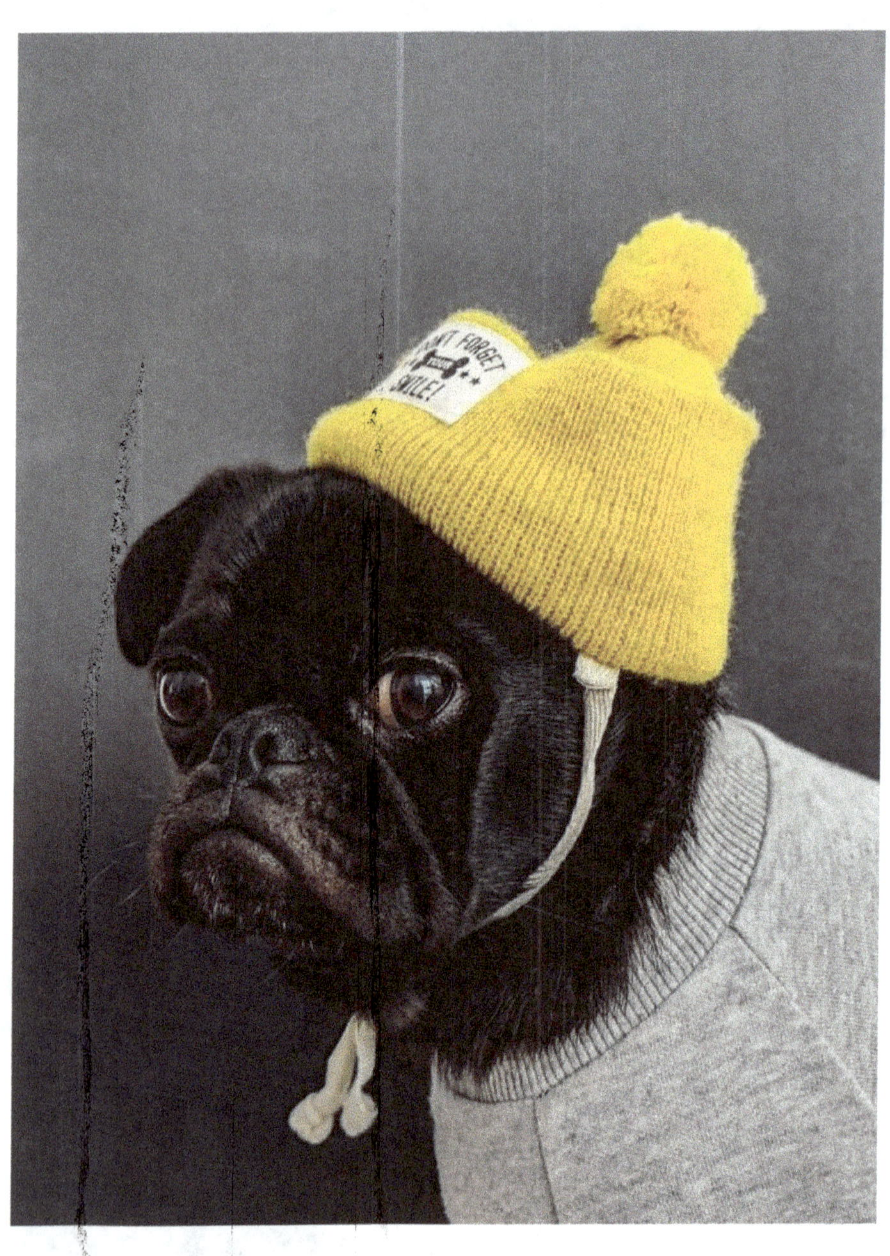

DON'T FORGET
YOUR
SMILE!

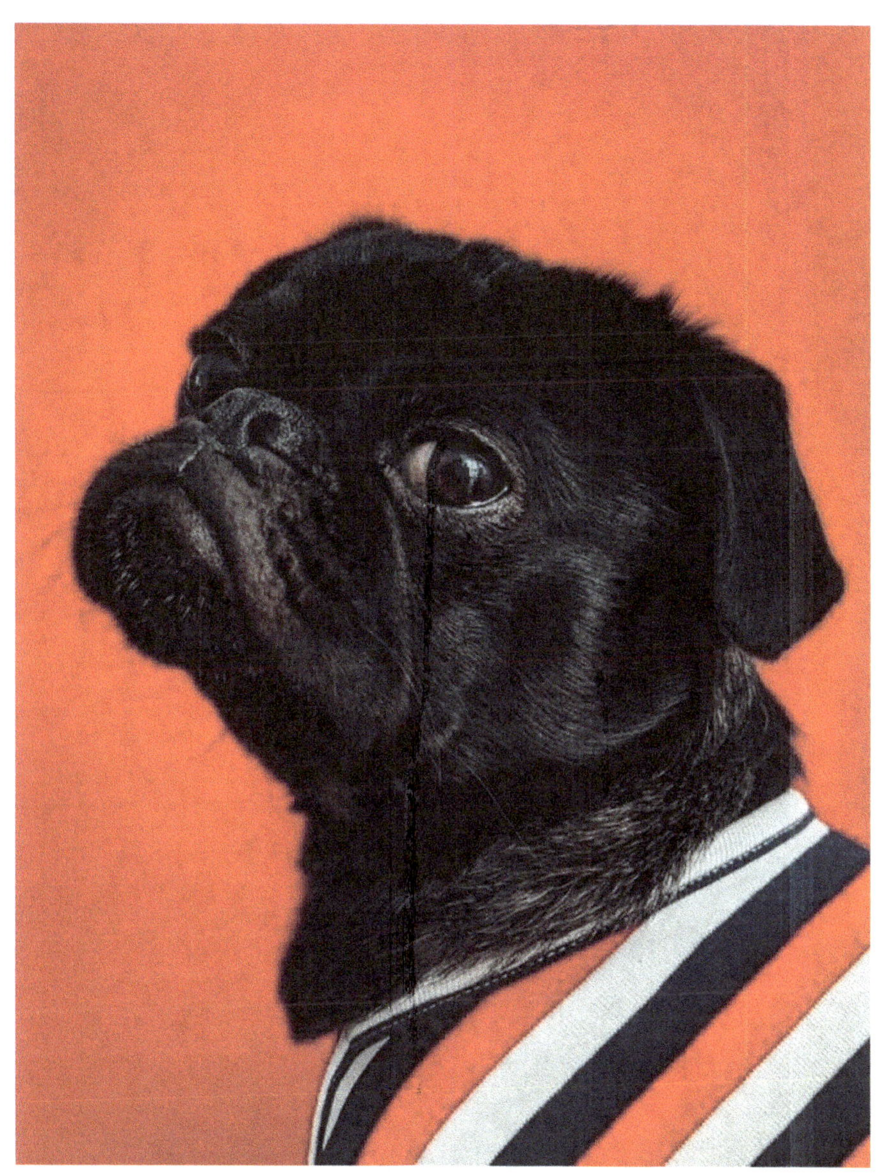

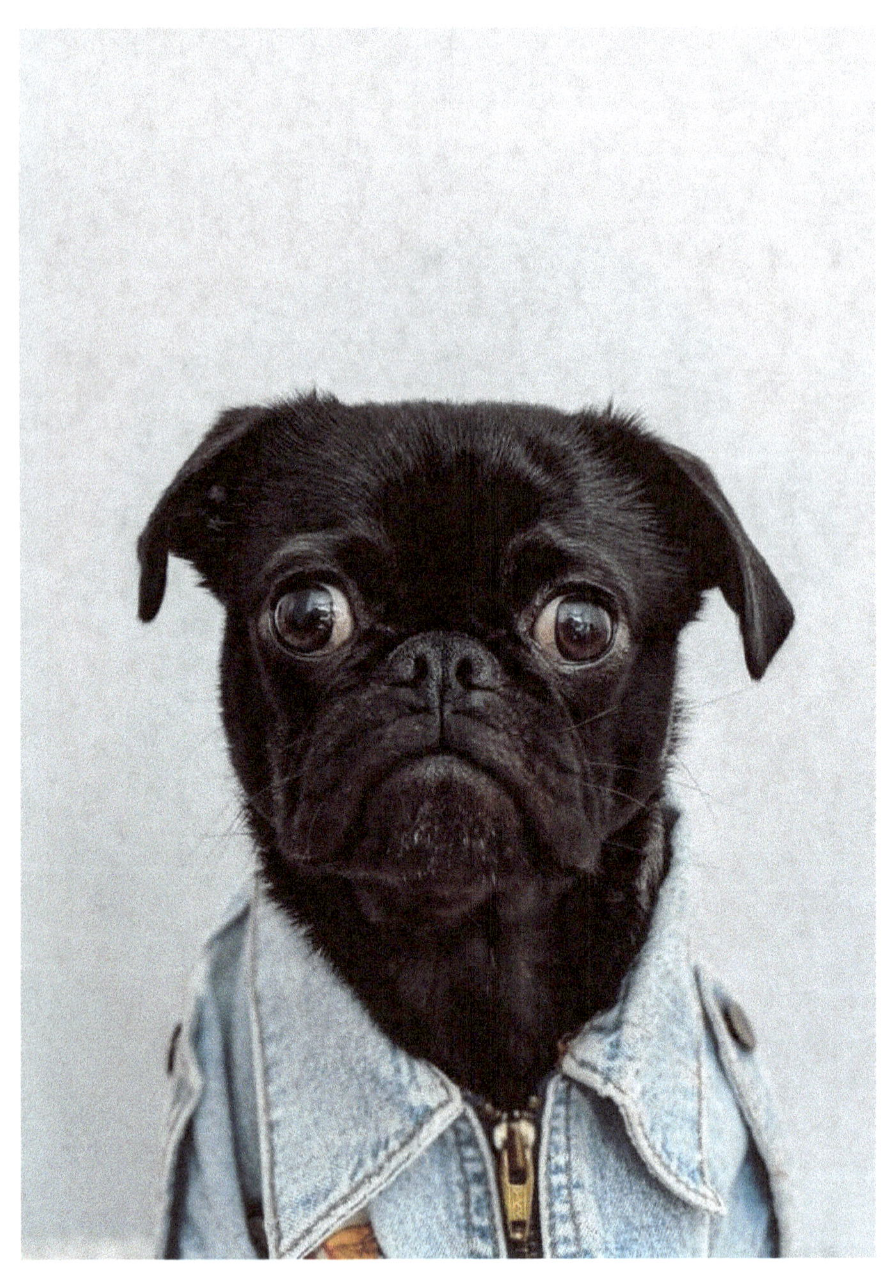

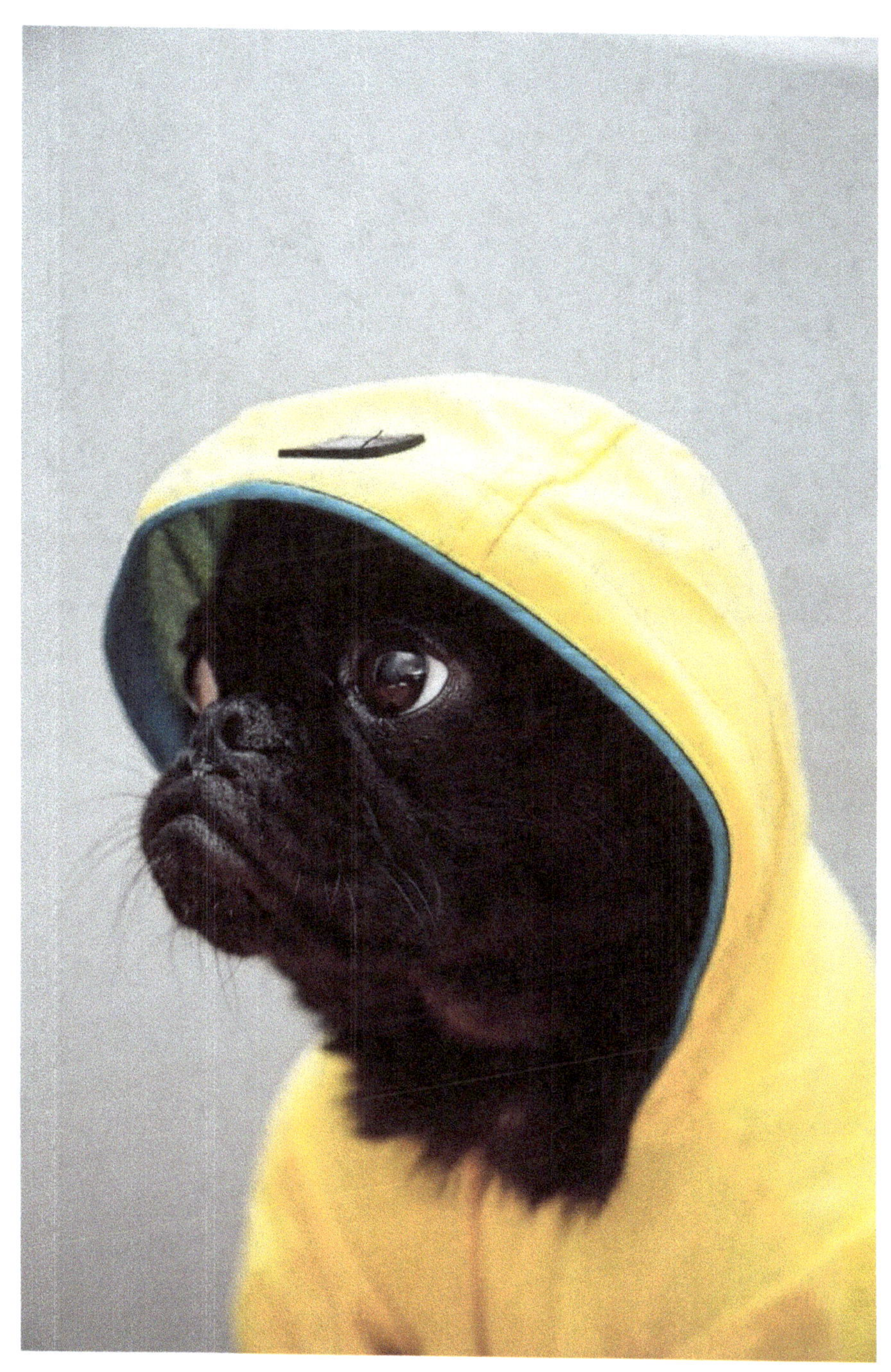

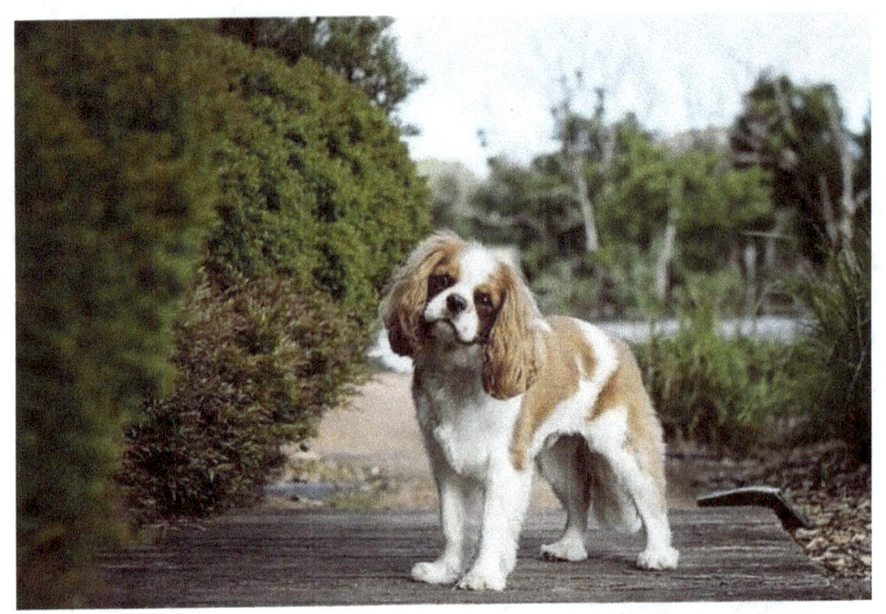

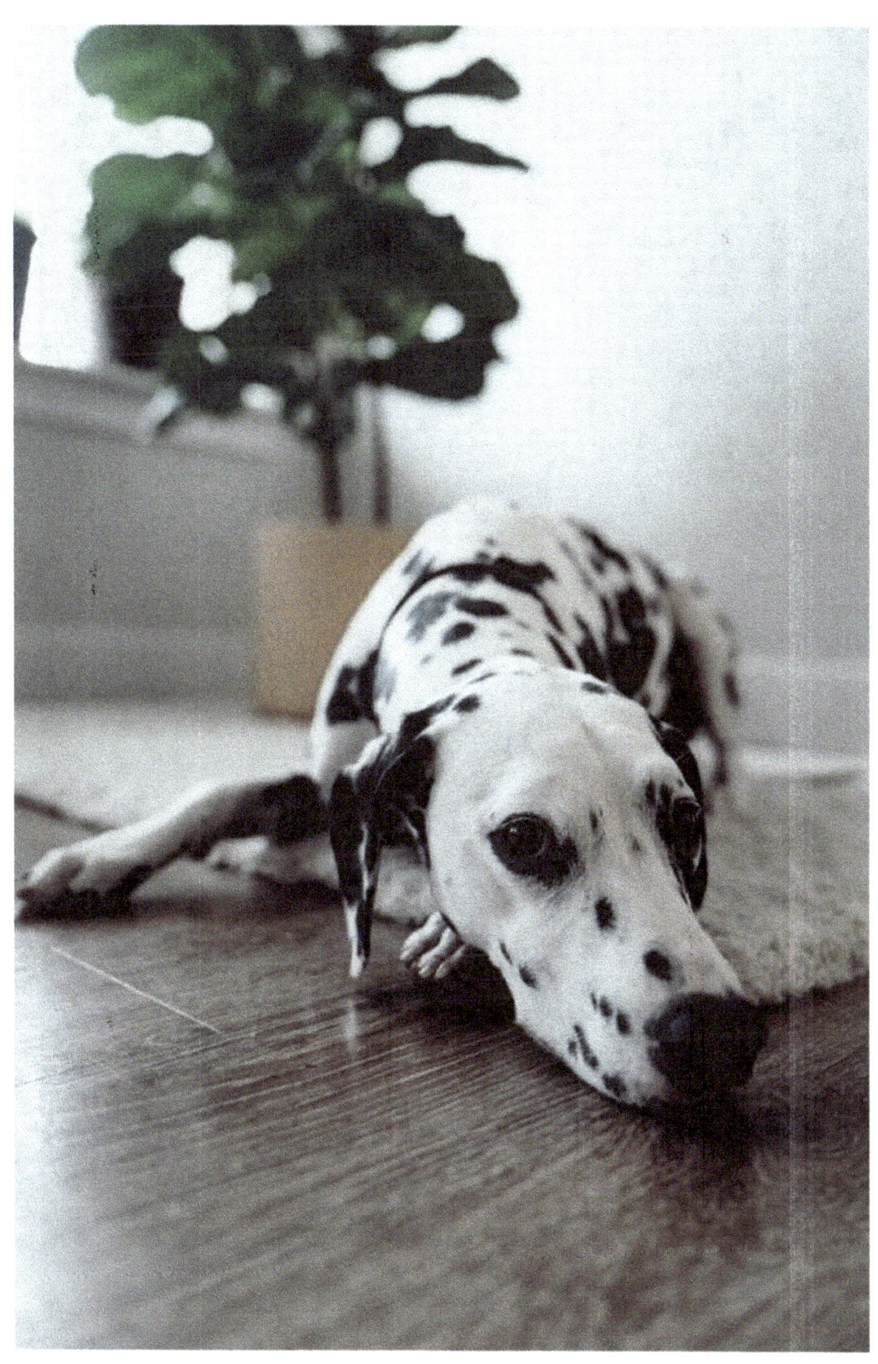

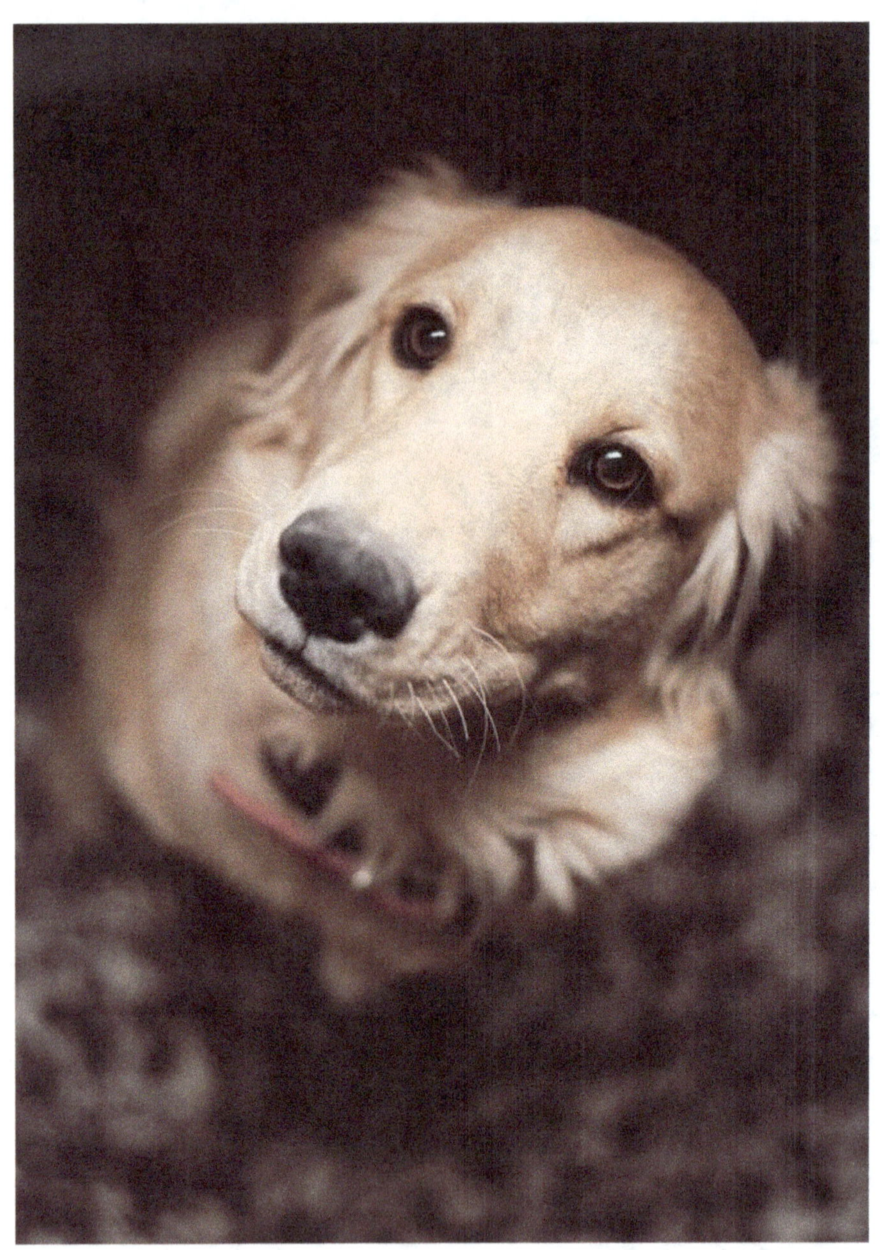

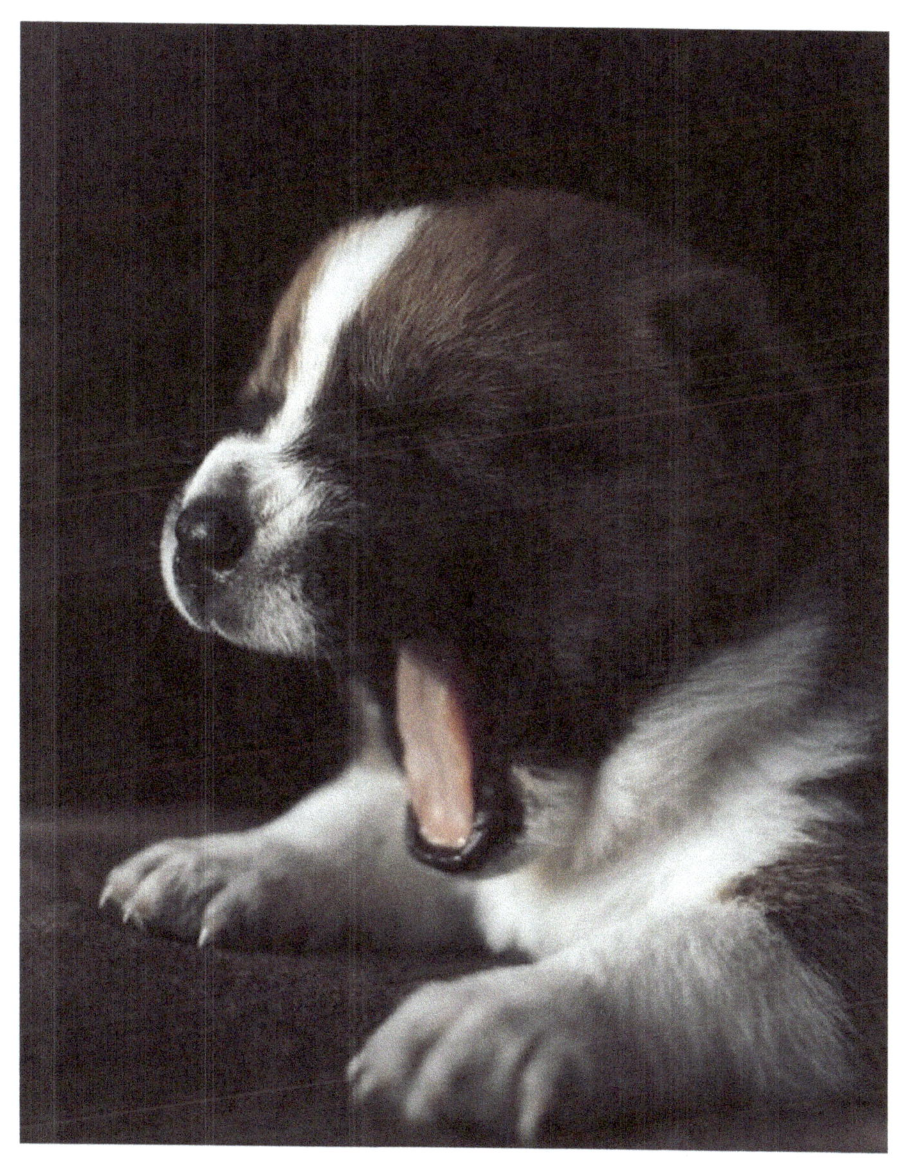

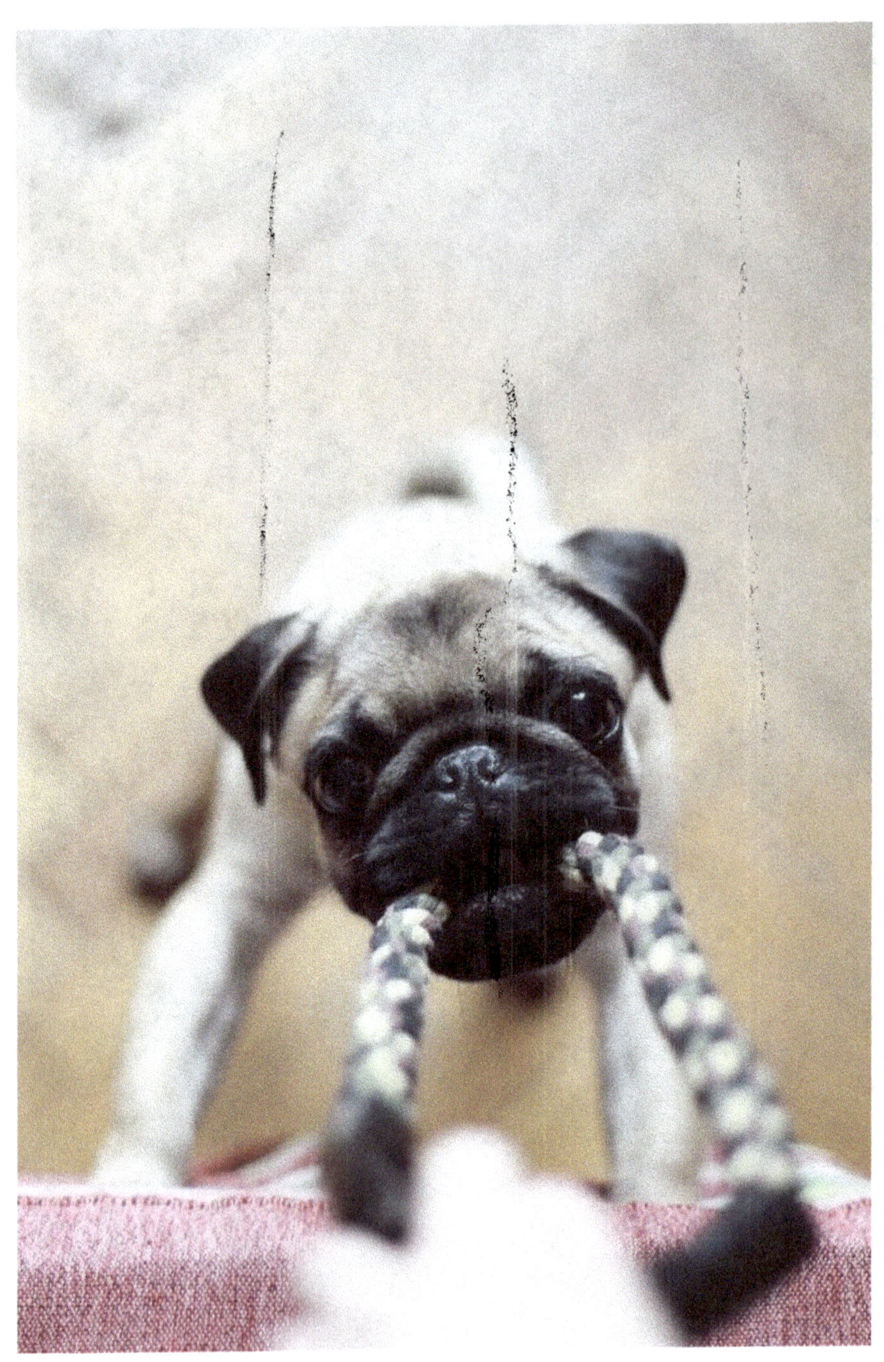

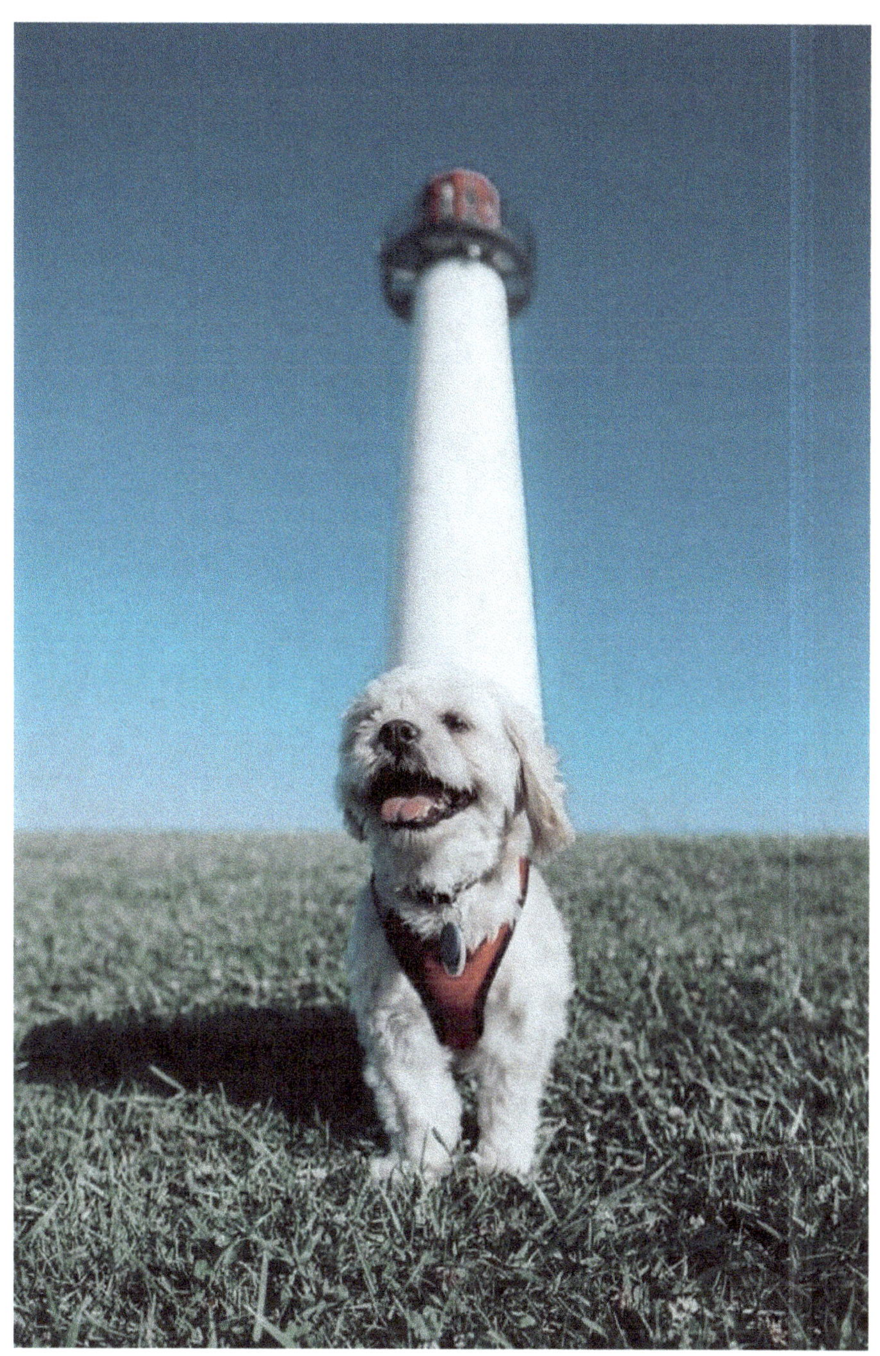

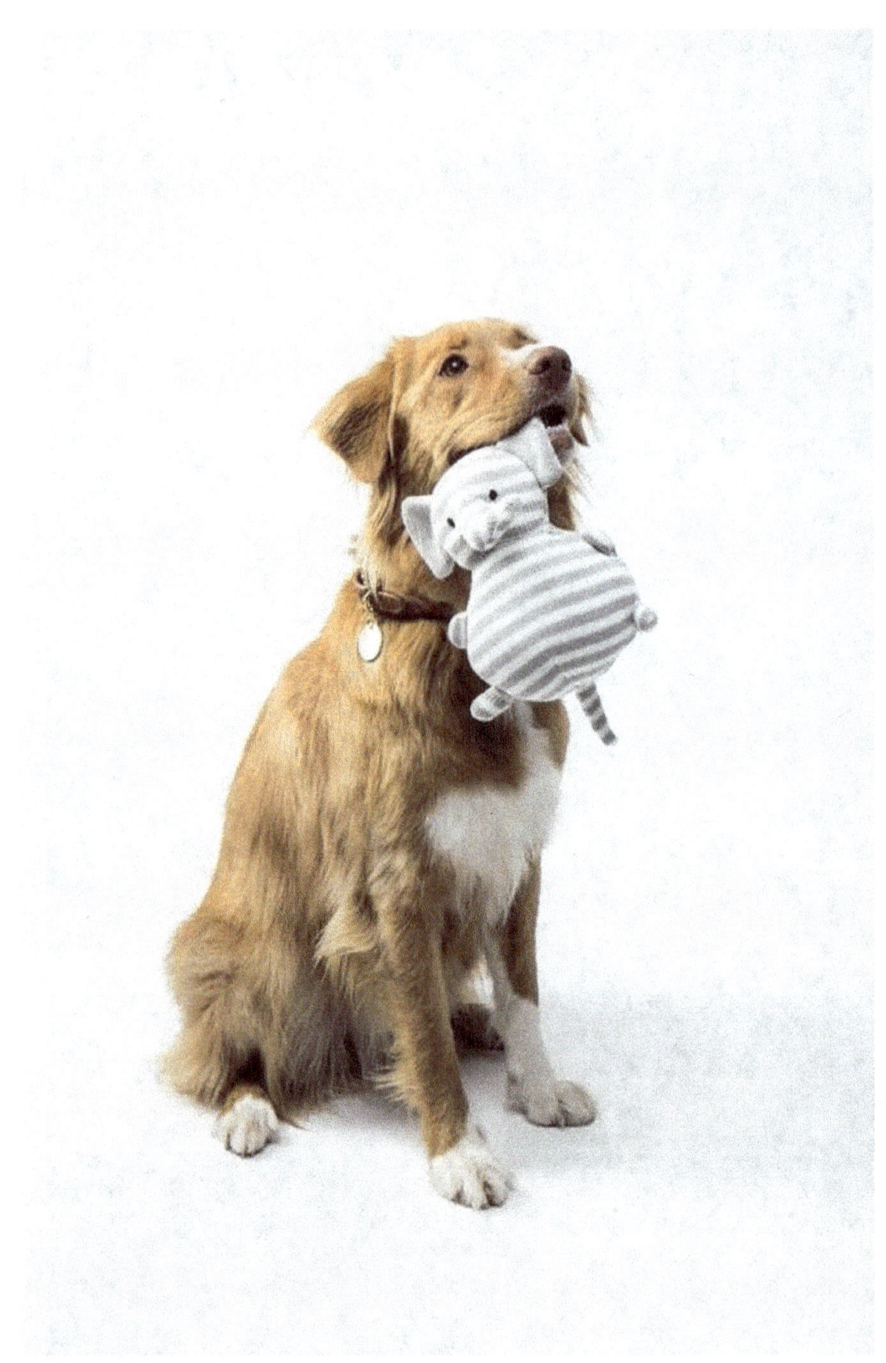

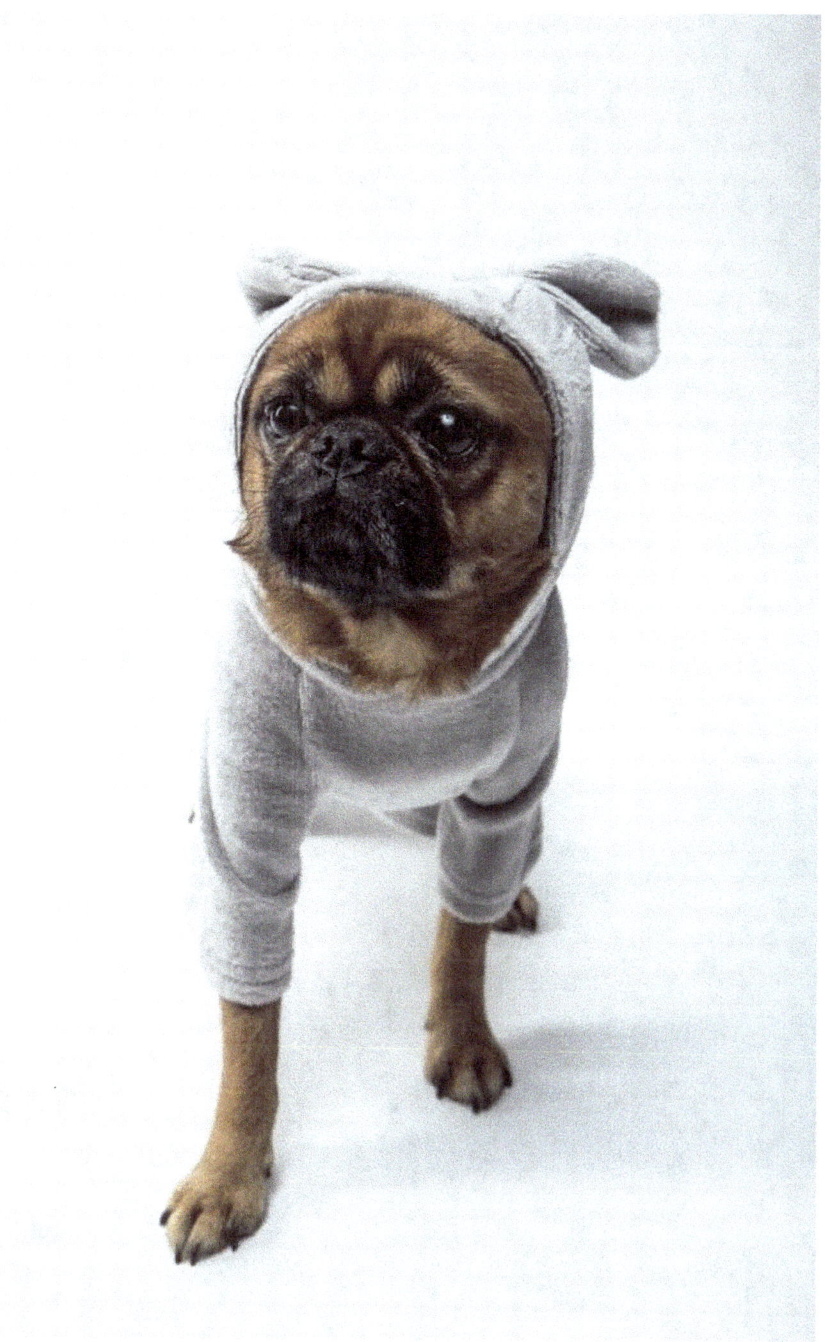

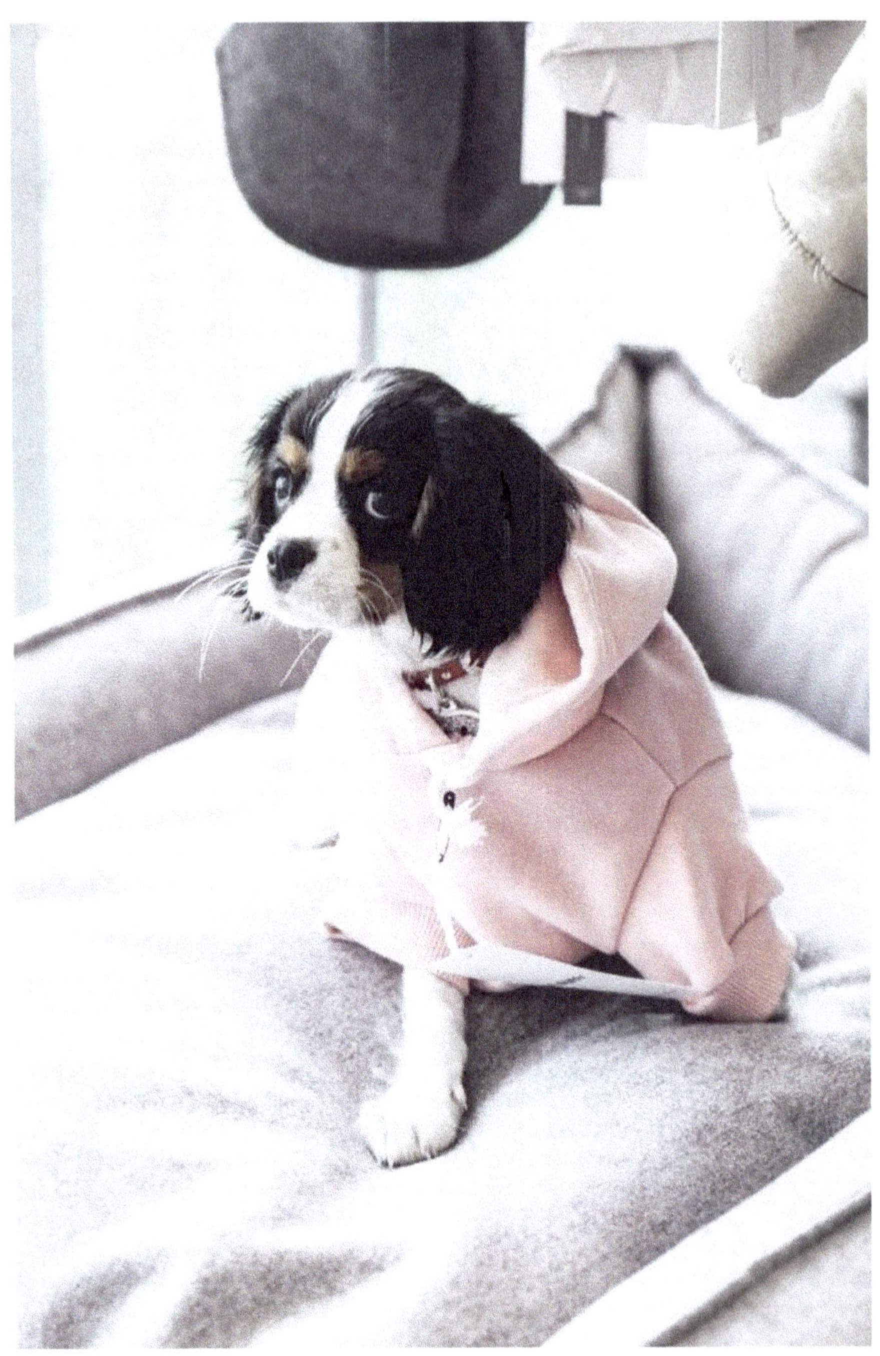

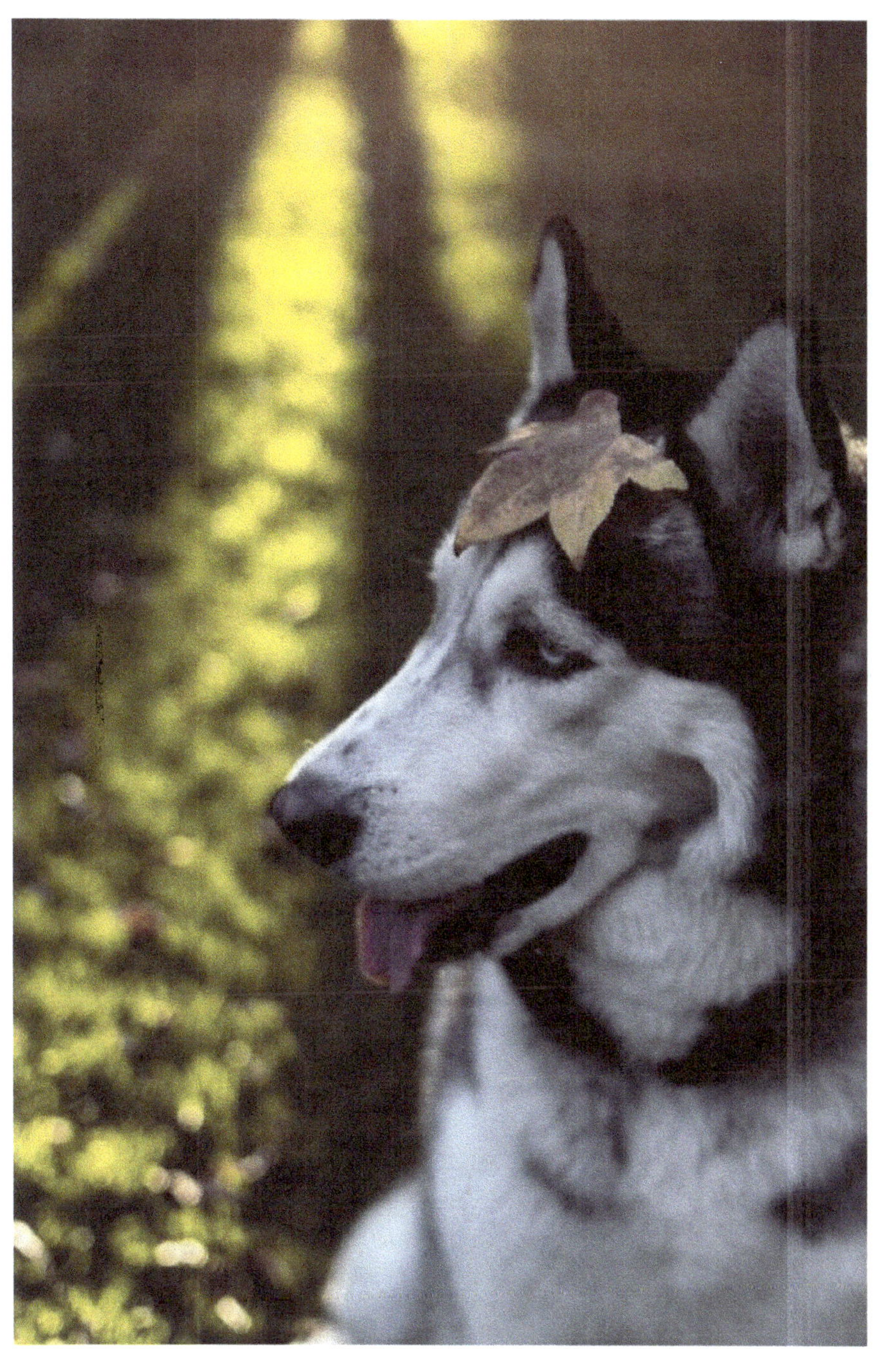

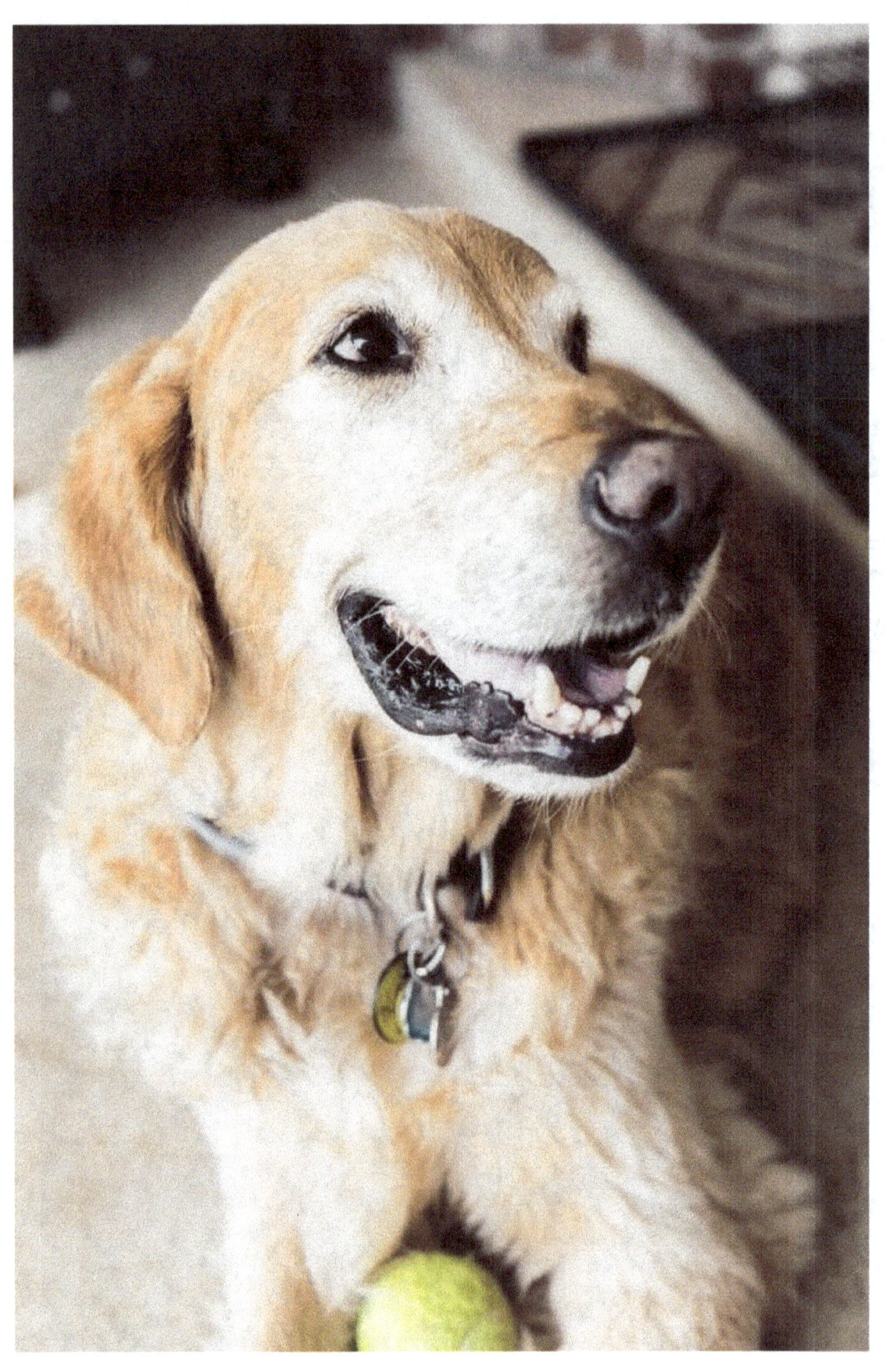

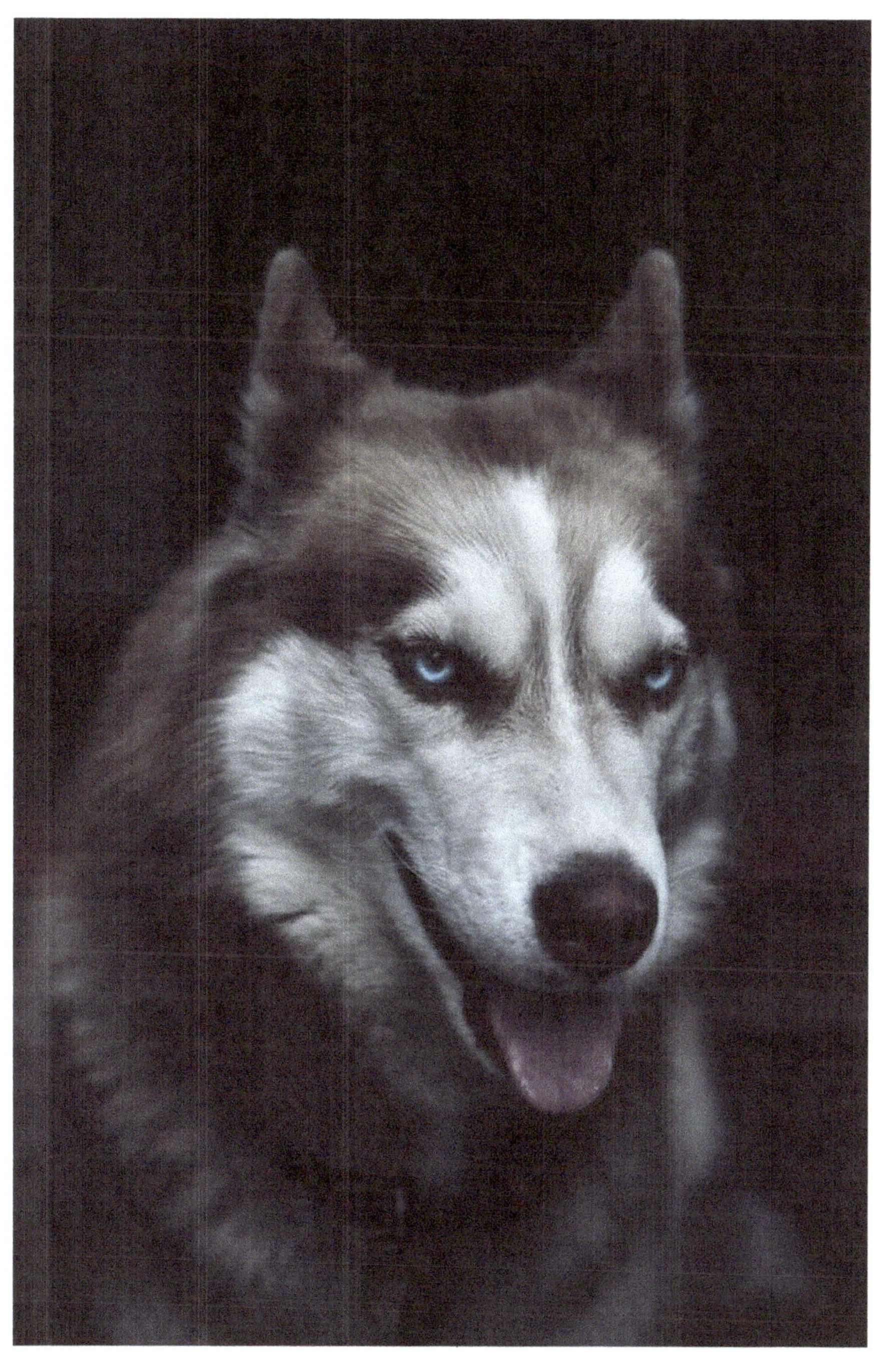

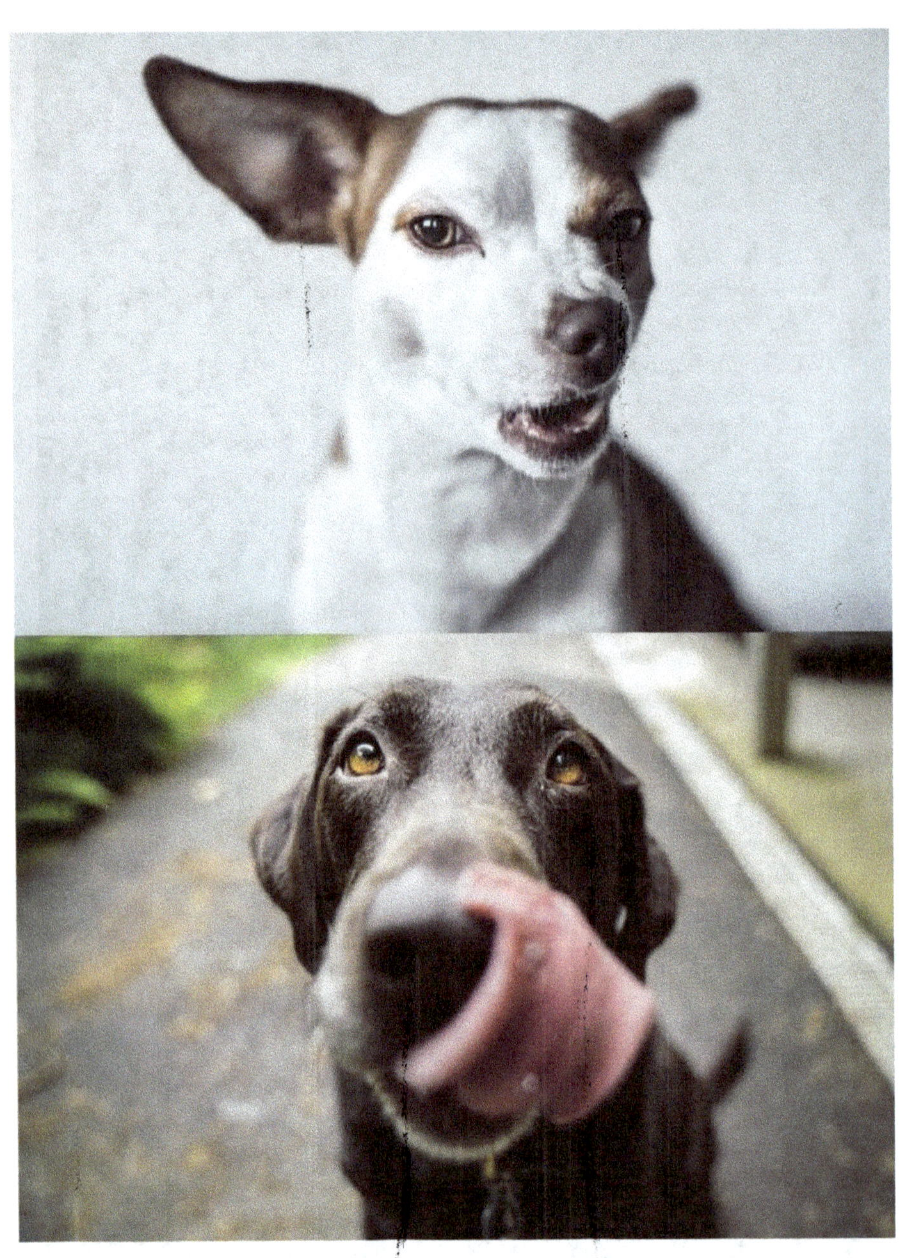

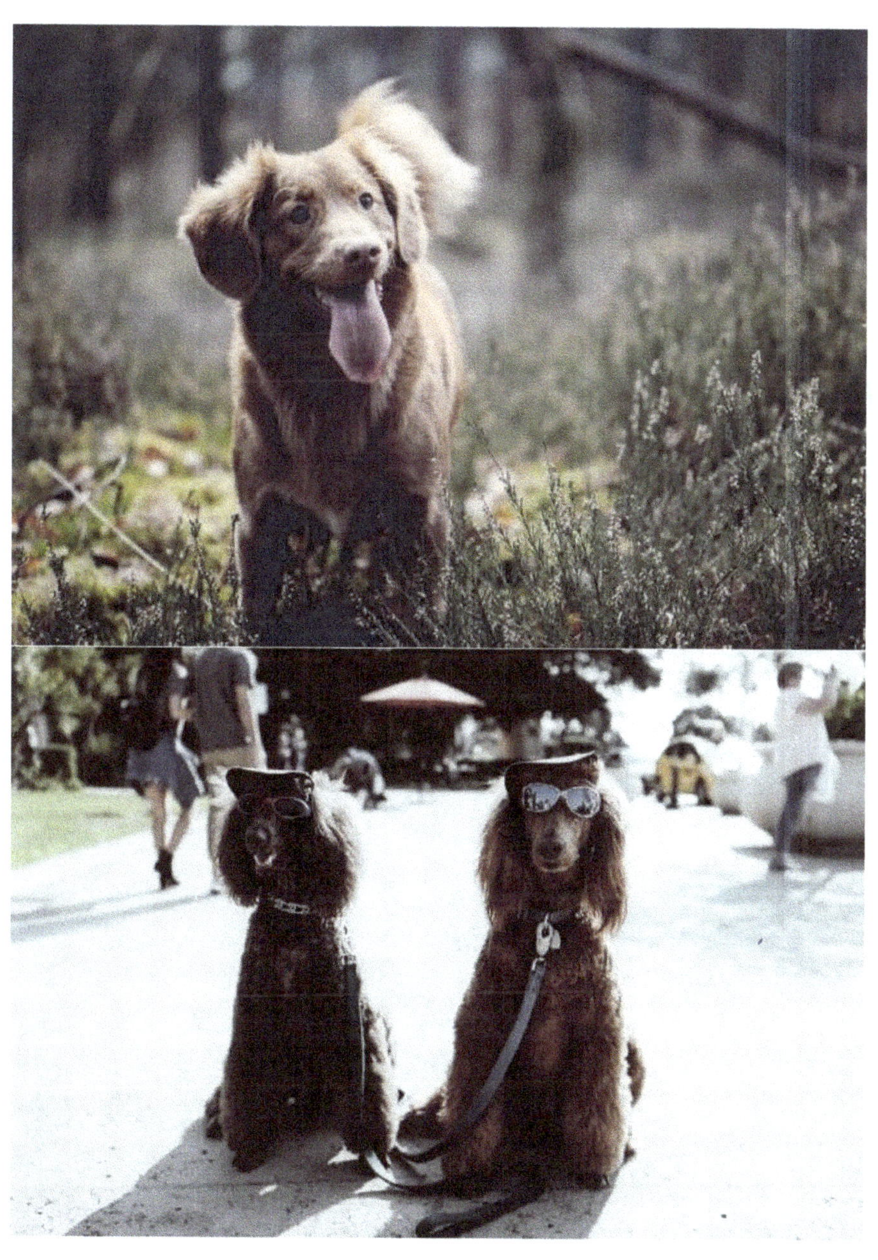

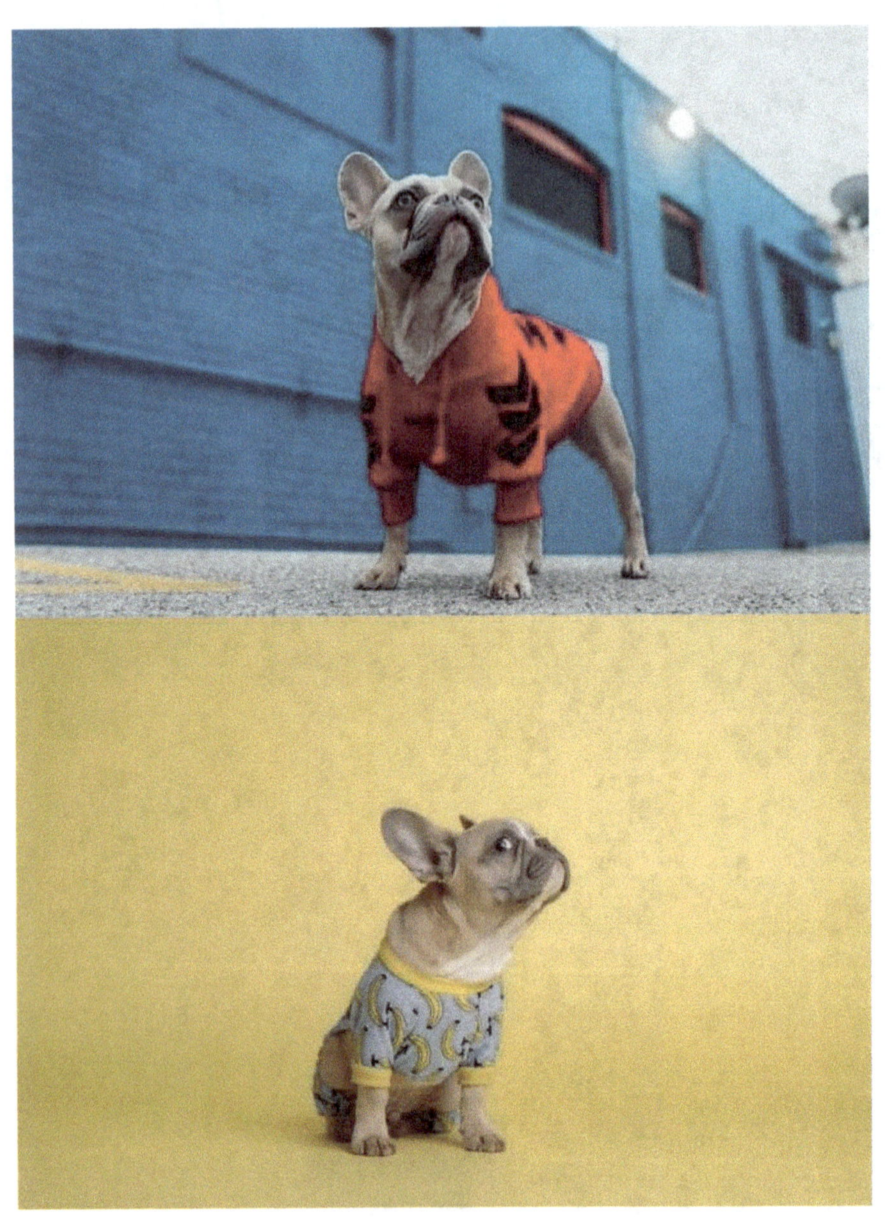

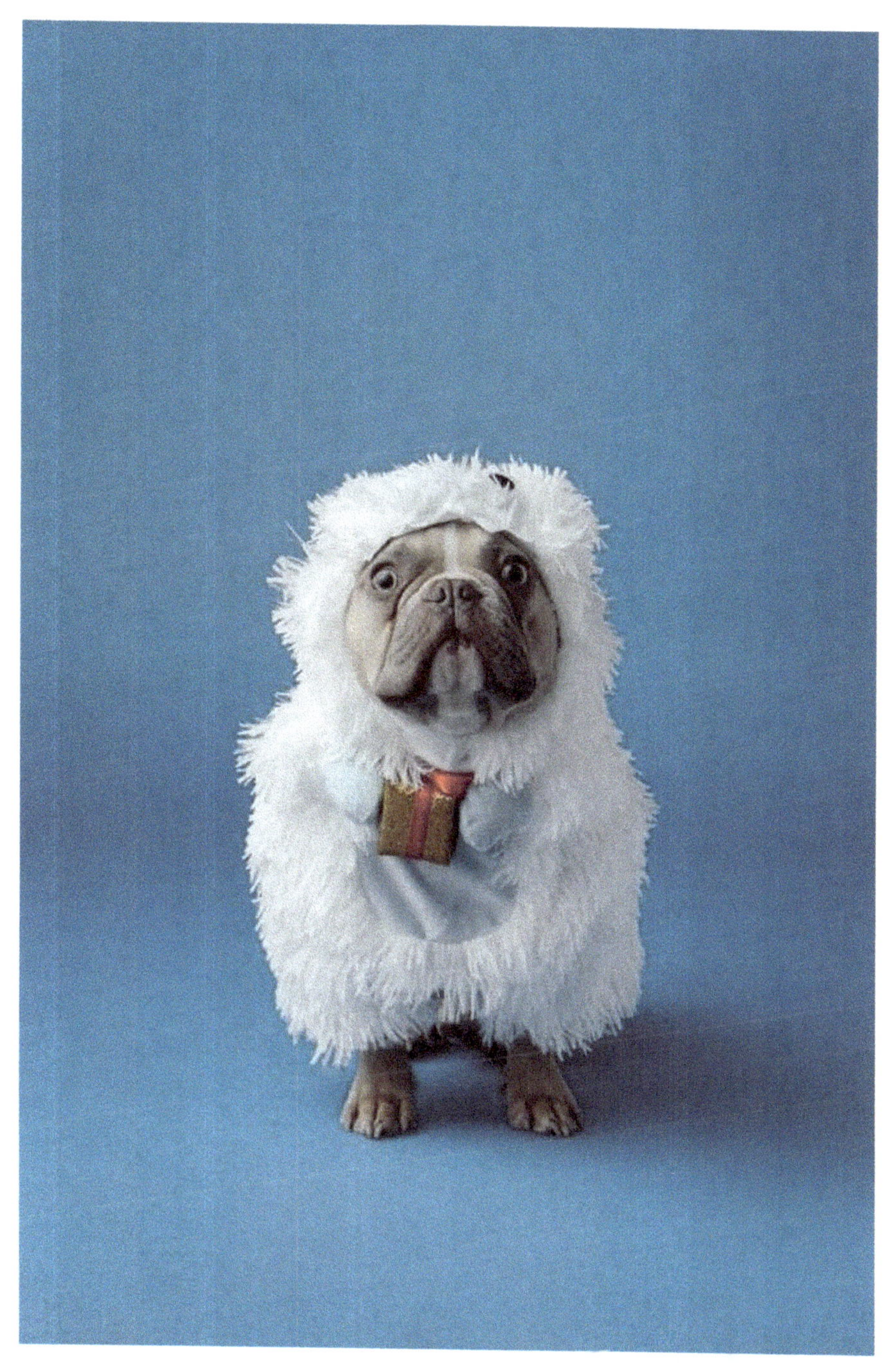

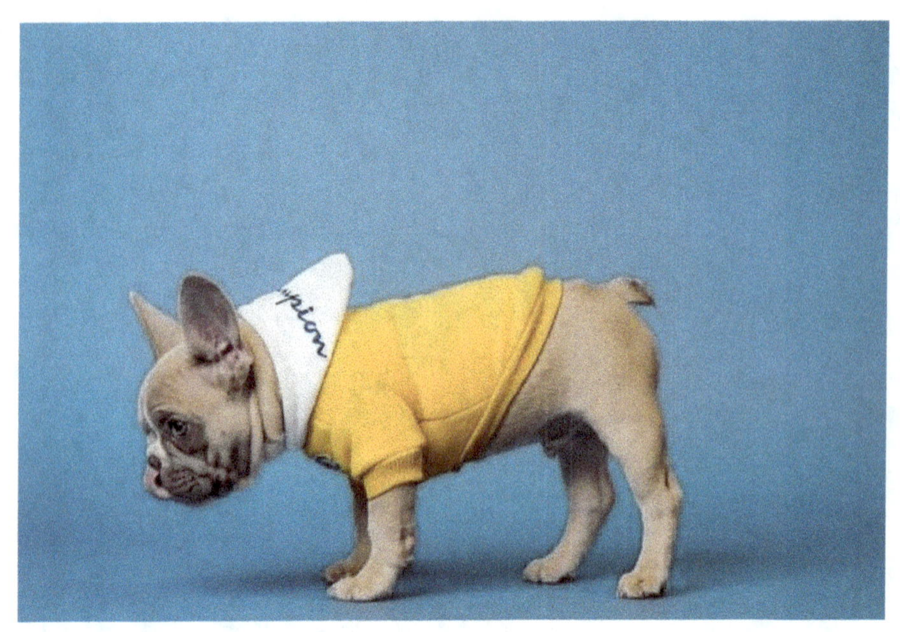
pion

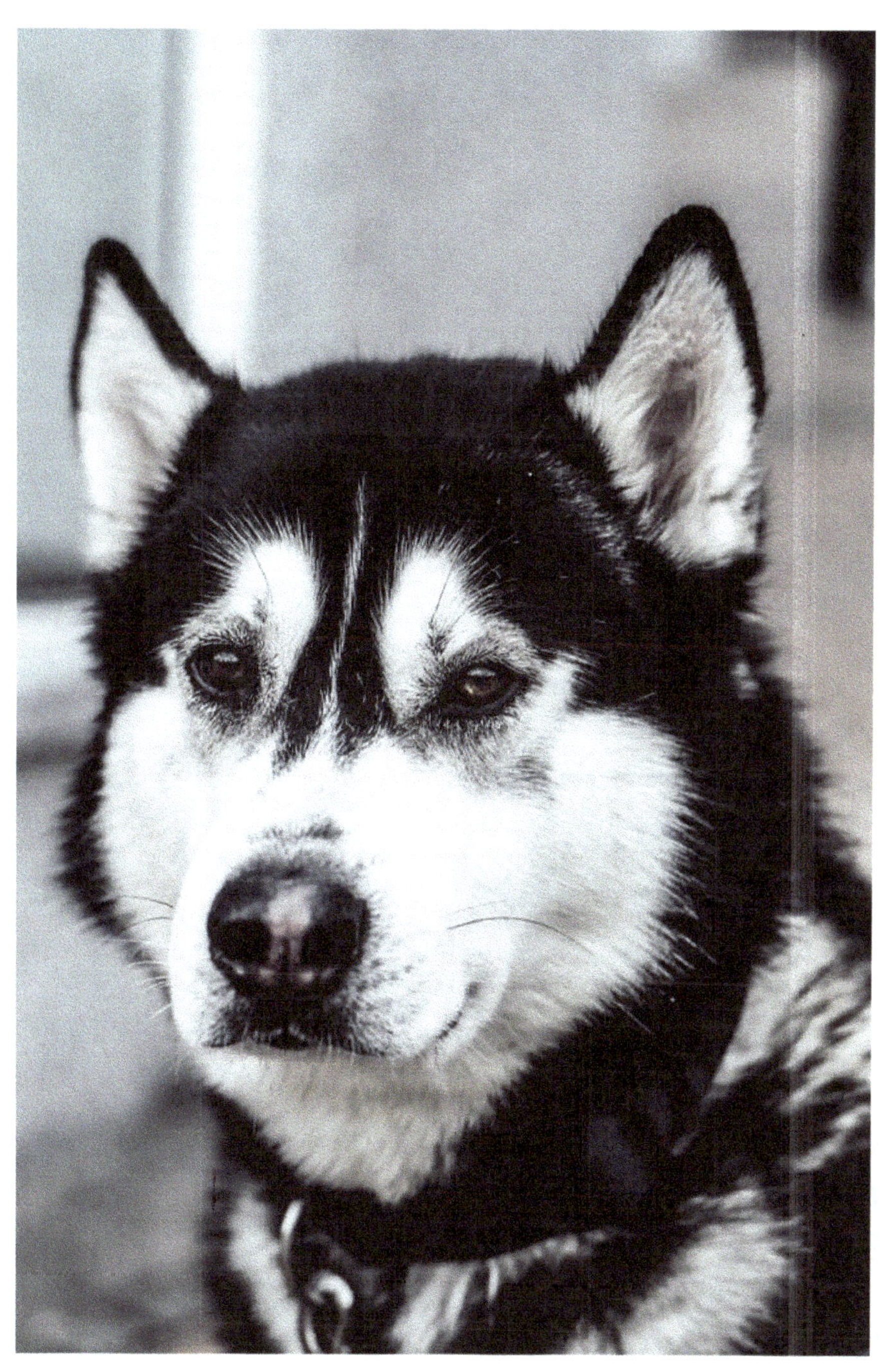

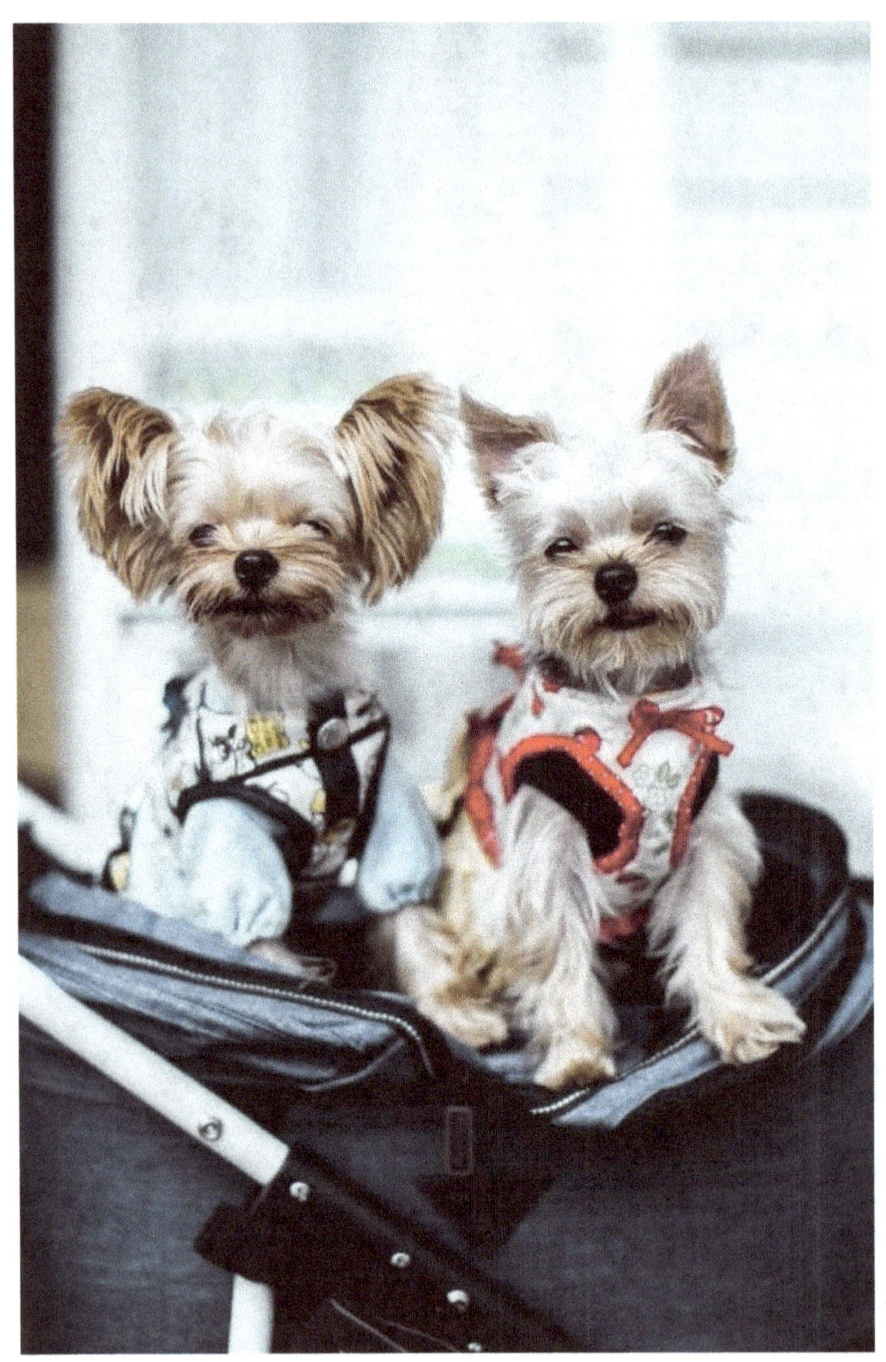

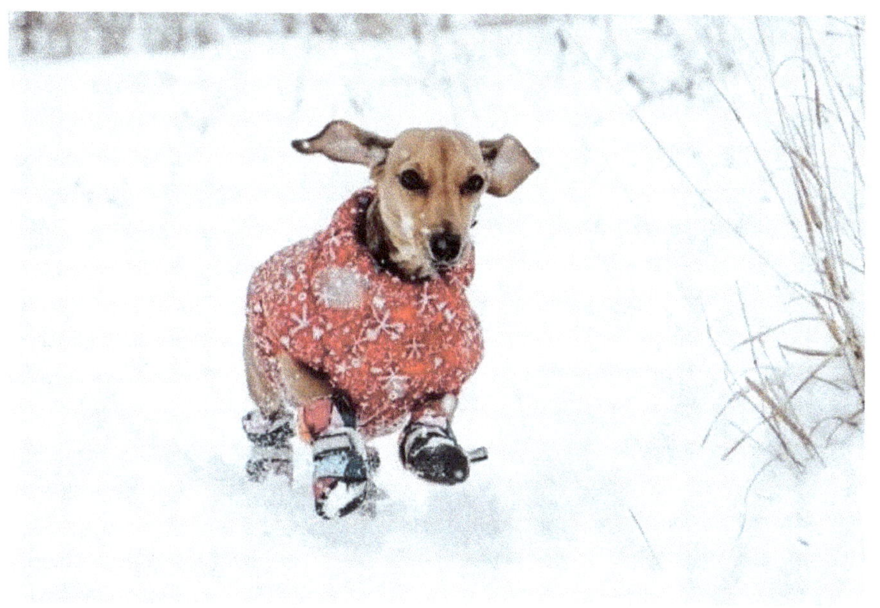

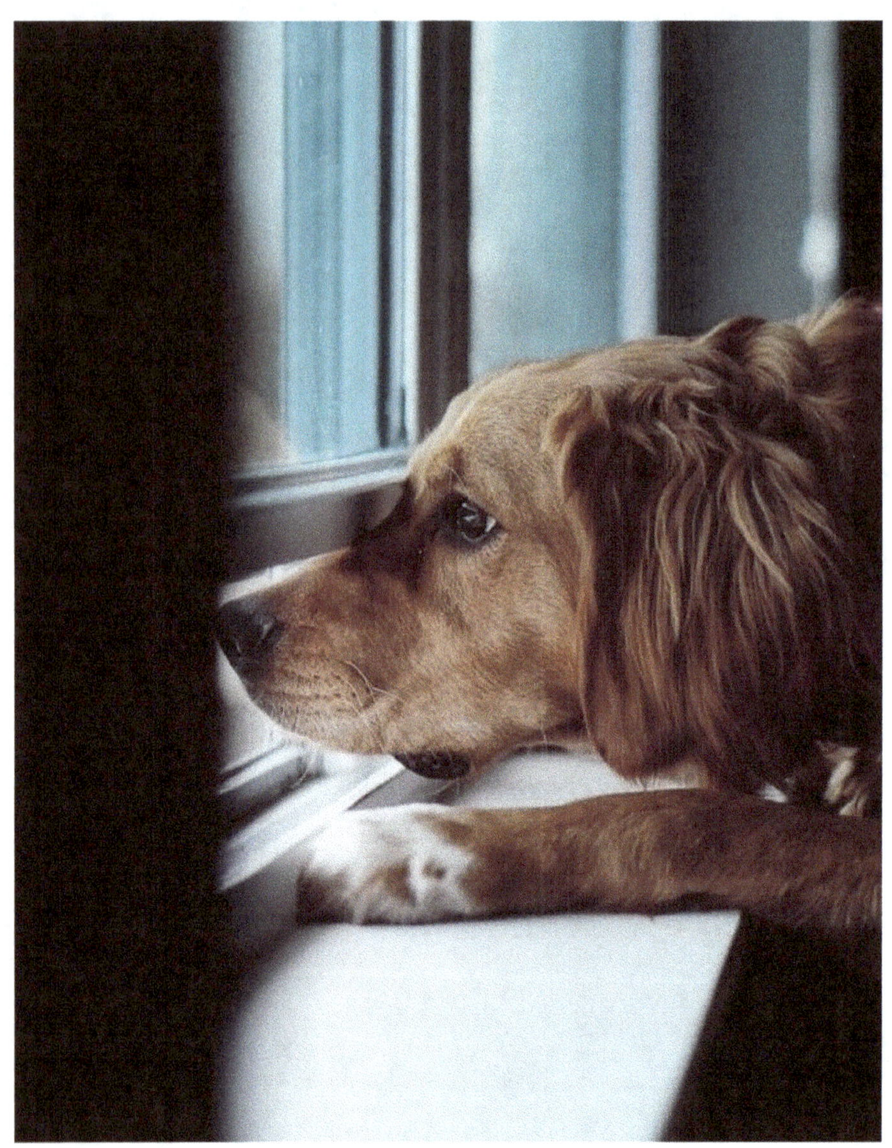

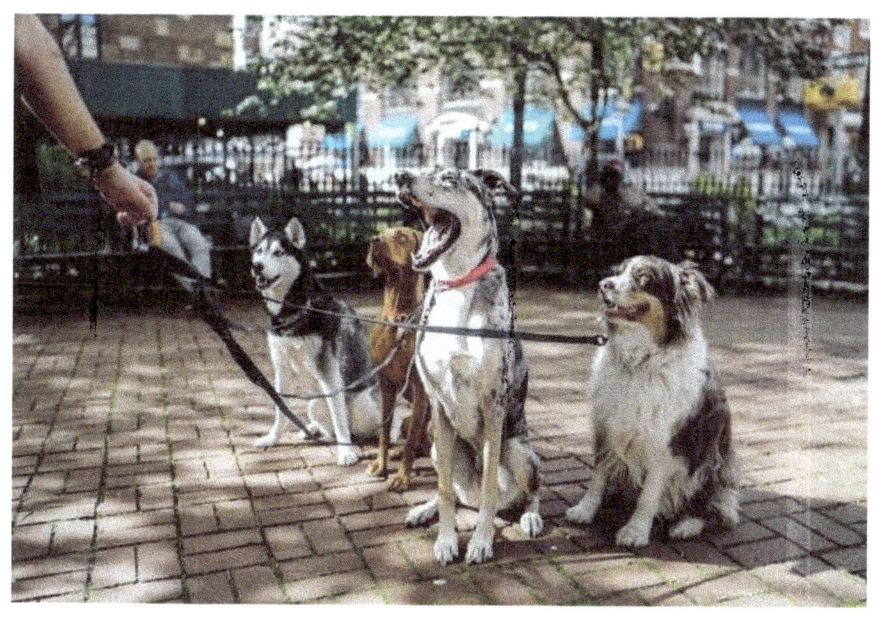

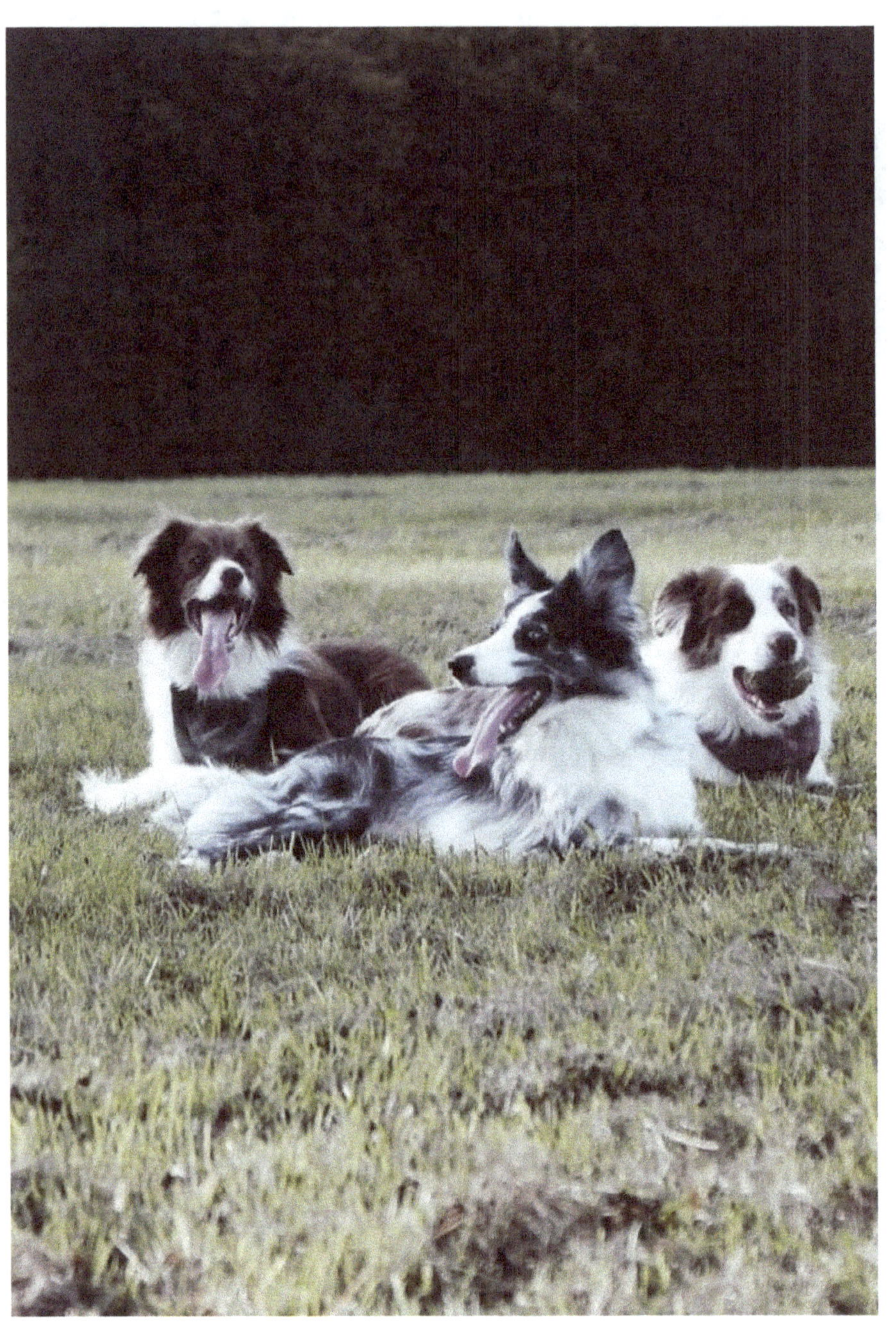

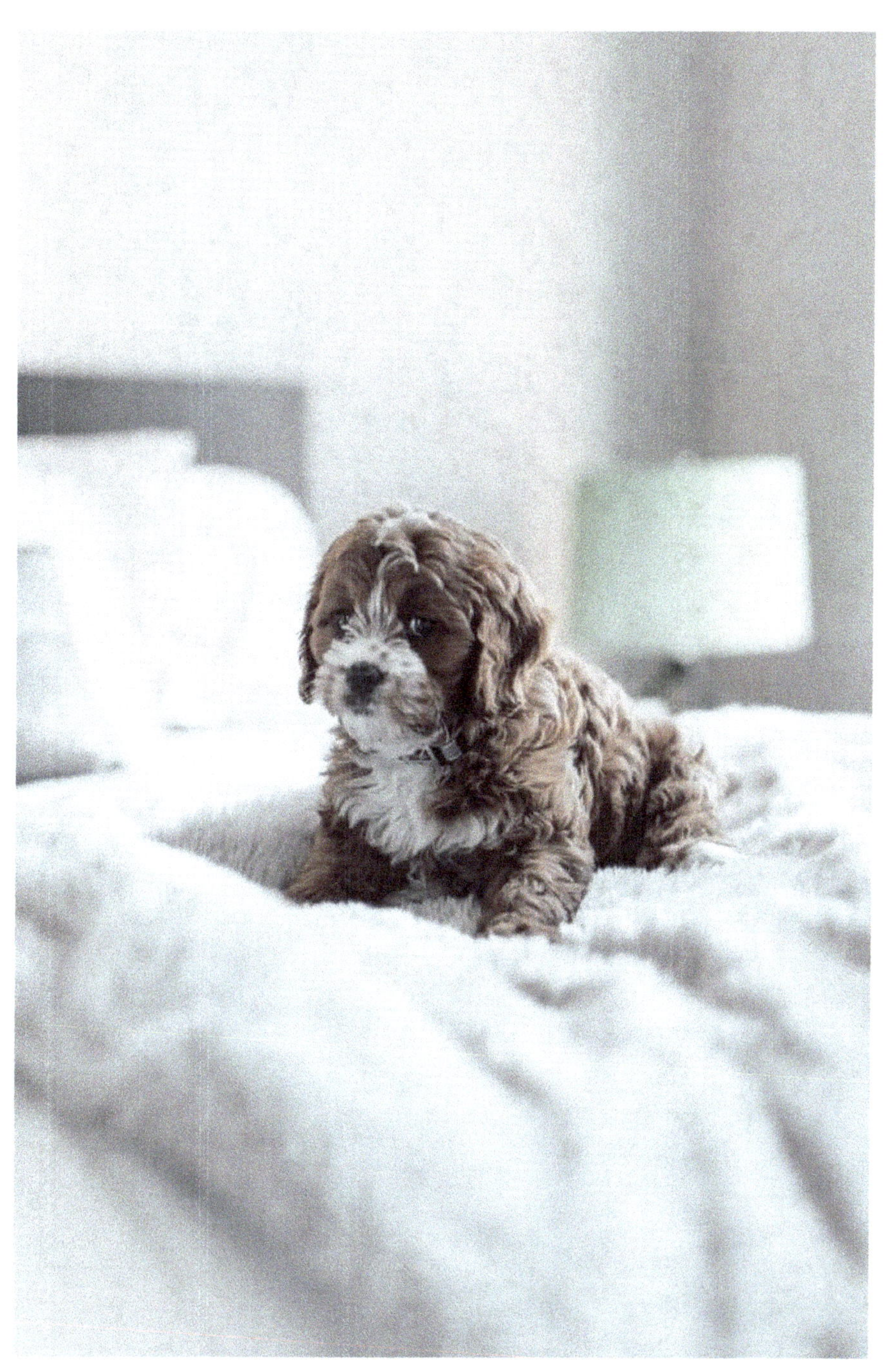

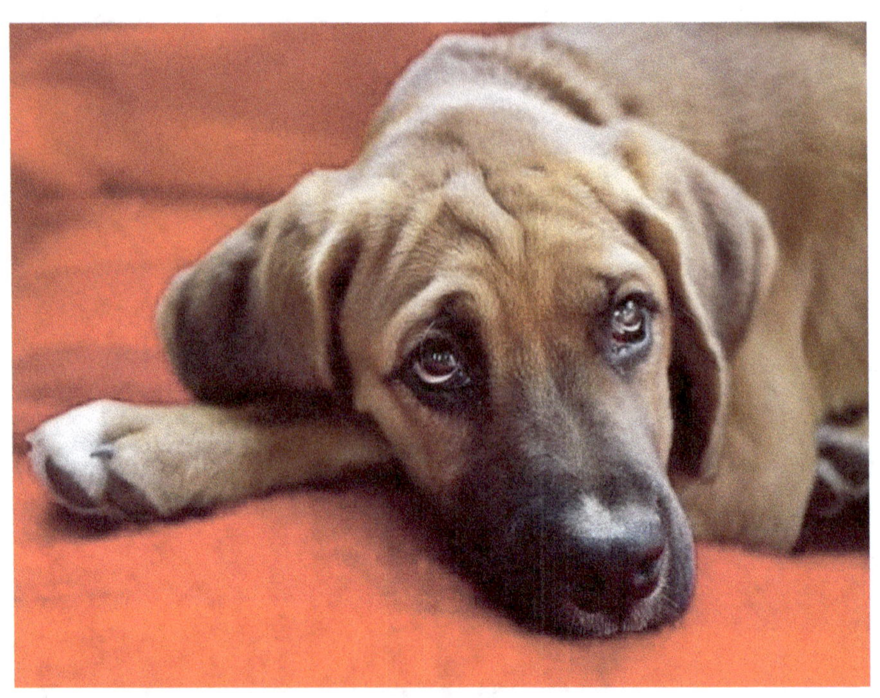

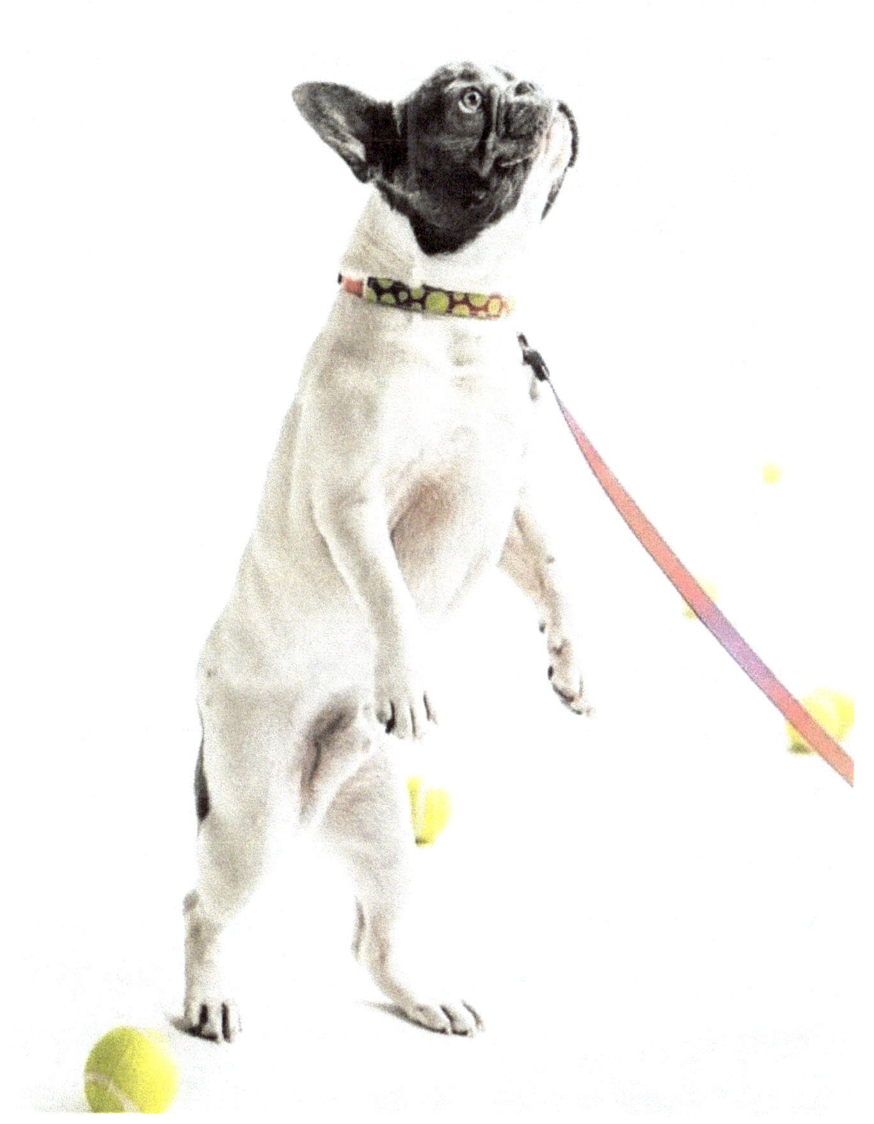

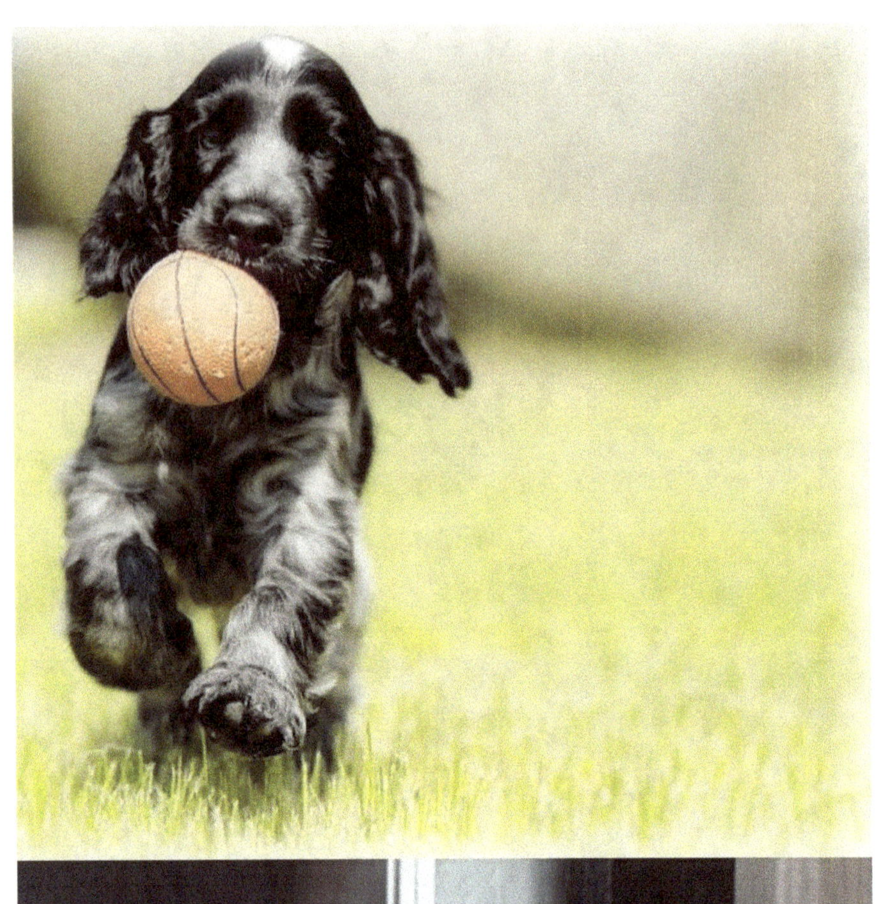

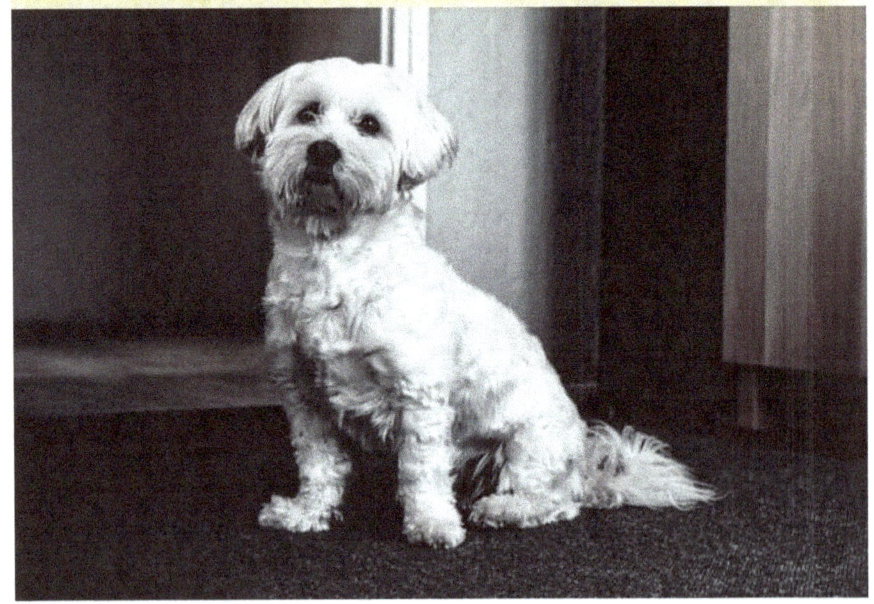

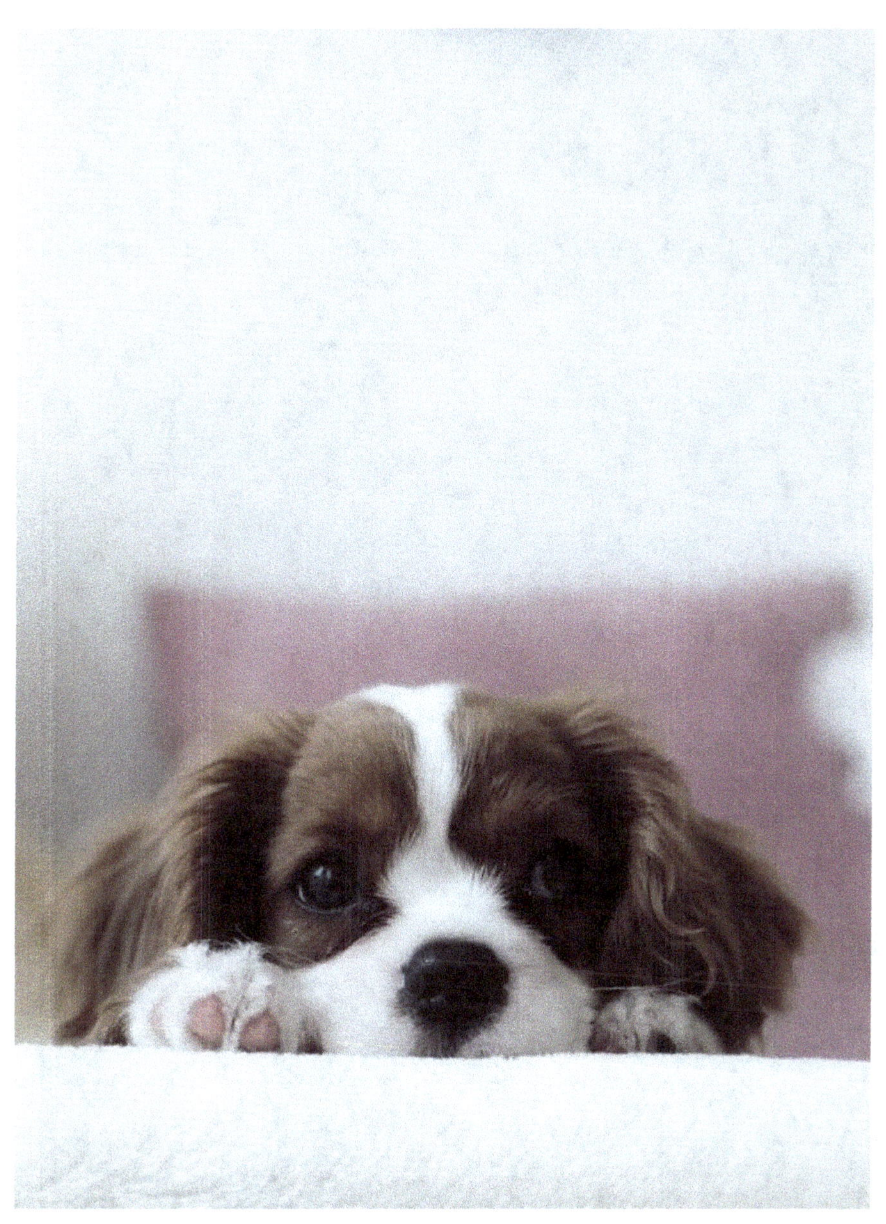

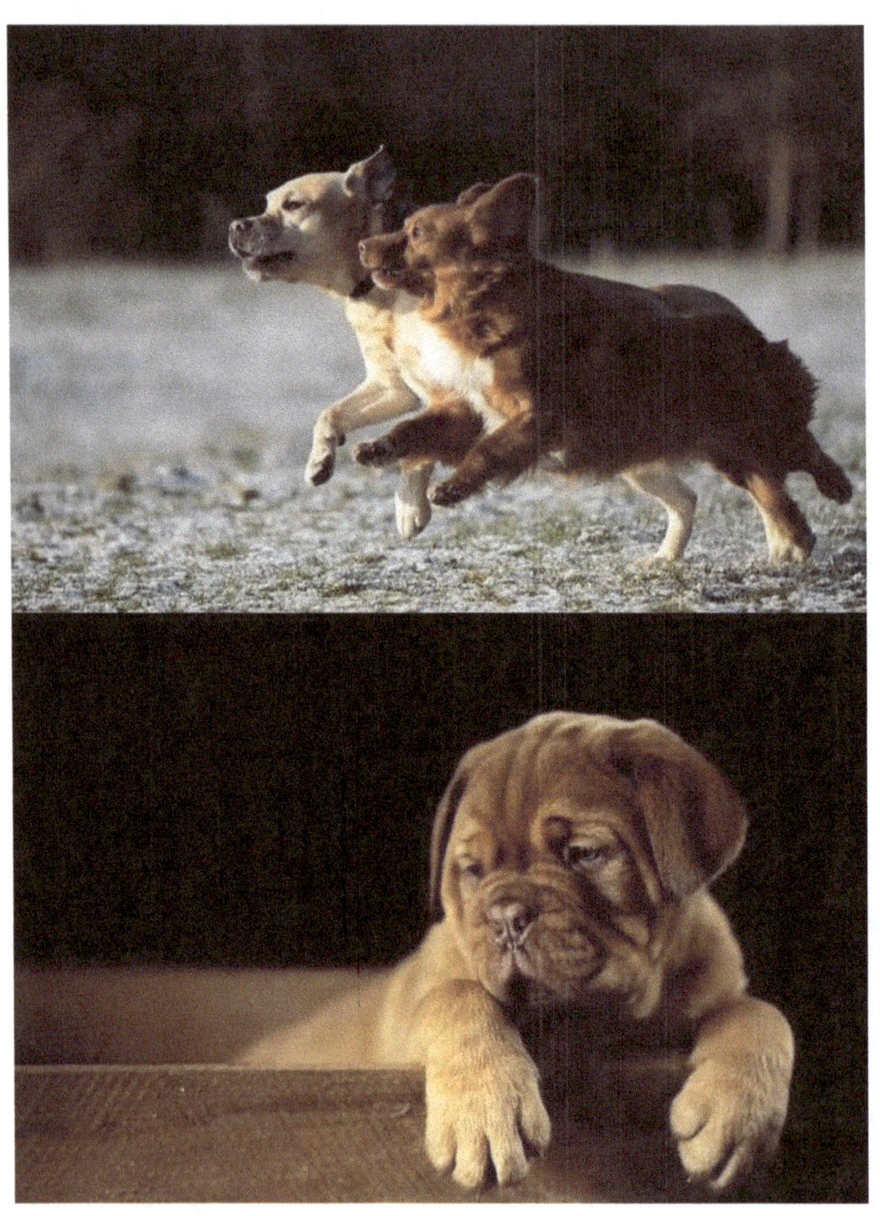

"The only creatures that are evolved enough to convey pure love are dogs and infants."

—*Johnny Depp*

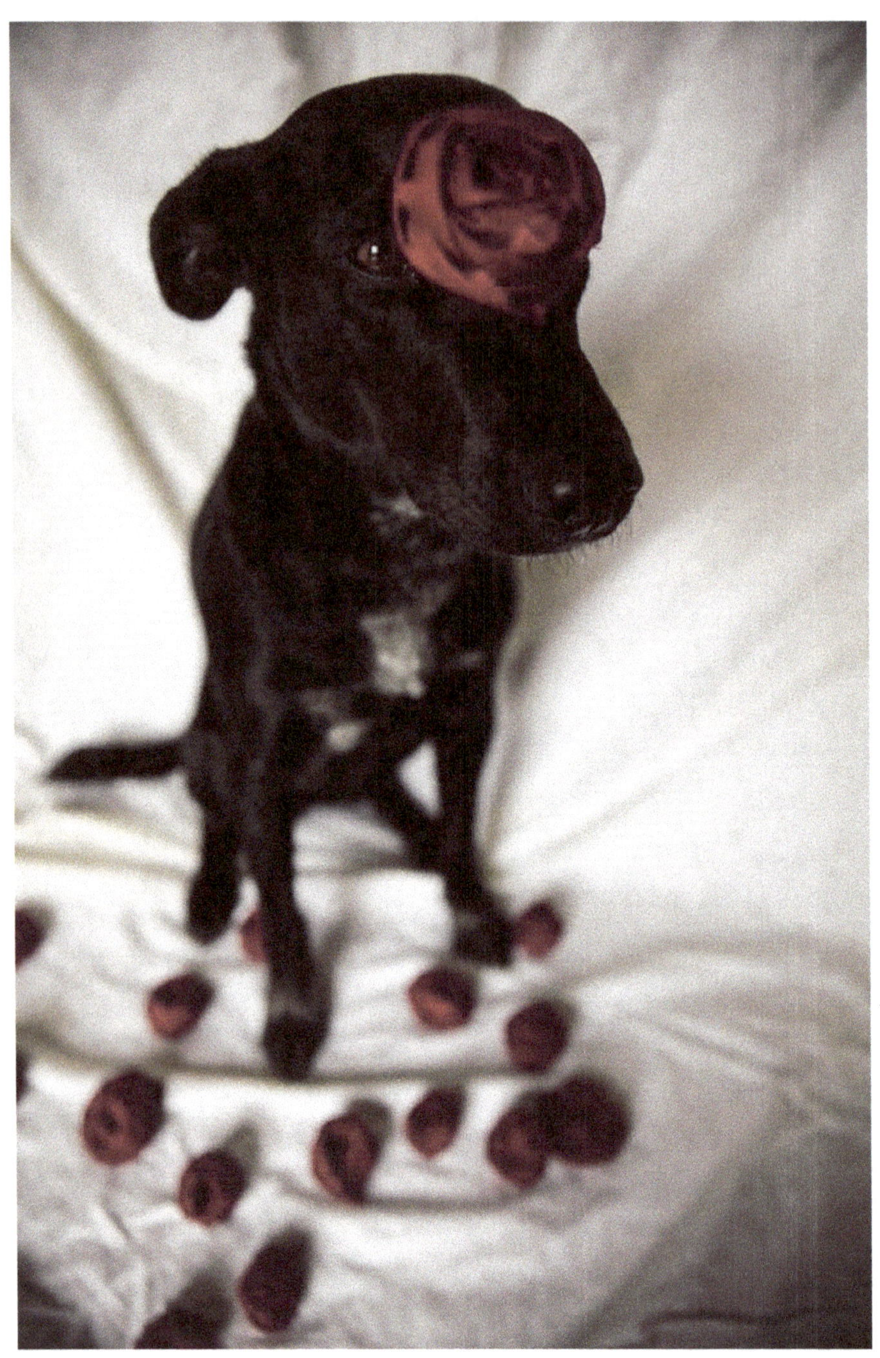